10

ECONOMIC ISSUES, PROBLEMS AND PERSPECTIVES

TAX RATES

ECONOMIC EFFECTS AND IMPLICATIONS

Economic Issues, Problems and Perspectives

Additional books in this series can be found on Nova's website under the Series tab.

Additional e-books in this series can be found on Nova's website under the e-books tab.

ECONOMIC ISSUES, PROBLEMS AND PERSPECTIVES

TAX RATES

ECONOMIC EFFECTS AND IMPLICATIONS

HOWARD P. DURHAM
EDITOR

NOVINKA
New York

For permission to use material from this book please contact us:
Telephone 631-231-7269; Fax 631-231-8175
Web Site: http://www.novapublishers.com

Library of Congress Cataloging-in-Publication Data

ISBN: 978-1-62417-215-1

Published by Nova Science Publishers, Inc. † New York

CONTENTS

PREFACE

Income tax rates have been at the center of recent policy debates over taxes. Some policymakers have argued that raising tax rates, especially on higher income taxpayers, to increase tax revenues is part of the solution for long-term debt reduction. For example, the Senate recently passed the Middle Class Tax Cut, which would allow the 2001 and 2003 Bush tax cuts to expire for taxpayers with income over $250,000. The Senate recently considered legislation, the Paying a Fair Share Act of 2012, that would implement the "Buffett rule" by raising the tax rate on millionaires. Other recent budget and deficit reduction proposals would reduce tax rates. This book examines individual income tax rates since 1945 in relation to these arguments and seeks to establish what, if any, relationship exists between the top tax rates and economic growth, using statistical analysis.

Chapter 1 – Income tax rates have been at the center of recent policy debates over taxes. Some policymakers have argued that raising tax rates, especially on higher income taxpayers, to increase tax revenues is part of the solution for long-term debt reduction. For example, the Senate recently passed the Middle Class Tax Cut (S. 3412), which would allow the 2001 and 2003 Bush tax cuts to expire for taxpayers with income over $250,000 ($200,000 for single taxpayers). The Senate recently considered legislation, the Paying a Fair Share Act of 2012 (S. 2230), that would implement the "Buffett rule" by raising the tax rate on millionaires. Other recent budget and deficit reduction proposals would reduce tax rates. The President's 2010 Fiscal Commission recommended reducing the budget deficit and tax rates by broadening the tax base—the additional revenues from broadening the tax base would be used for deficit reduction and tax rate reductions. The plan advocated by House Budget Committee Chairman Paul Ryan that is embodied in the House Budget

Resolution (H.Con.Res. 112), the *Path to Prosperity*, also proposes to reduce income tax rates by broadening the tax base. Both plans would broaden the tax base by reducing or eliminating tax expenditures. Advocates of lower tax rates argue that reduced rates would increase economic growth, increase saving and investment, and boost productivity (increase the economic pie). Proponents of higher tax rates argue that higher tax revenues are necessary for debt reduction, that tax rates on the rich are too low (i.e., they violate the Buffett rule), and that higher tax rates on the rich would moderate increasing income inequality (change how the economic pie is distributed). This report attempts to clarify whether or not there is an association between the tax rates of the highest income taxpayers and economic growth. Data is analyzed to illustrate the association between the tax rates of the highest income taxpayers and measures of economic growth. Throughout the late-1940s and 1950s, the top marginal tax rate was typically above 90%; today it is 35%. Additionally, the top capital gains tax rate was 25% in the 1950s and 1960s, 35% in the 1970s; today it is 15%. The real GDP growth rate averaged 4.2% and real per capita GDP increased annually by 2.4% in the 1950s. In the 2000s, the average real GDP growth rate was 1.7% and real per capita GDP increased annually by less than 1%. There is not conclusive evidence, however, to substantiate a clear relationship between the 65-year steady reduction in the top tax rates and economic growth. Analysis of such data suggests the reduction in the top tax rates have had little association with saving, investment, or productivity growth. However, the top tax rate reductions appear to be associated with the increasing concentration of income at the top of the income distribution. The share of income accruing to the top 0.1% of U.S. families increased from 4.2% in 1945 to 12.3% by 2007 before falling to 9.2% due to the 2007-2009 recession. The evidence does not suggest necessarily a relationship between tax policy with regard to the top tax rates and the size of the economic pie, but there may be a relationship to how the economic pie is sliced. The U.S. unemployment rate has been over 8% since February 2009 and the Blue Chip consensus forecast has it remaining above 8% throughout 2012. In addition, if current fiscal policies continue, the United States could be facing a debt level approaching 200% of gross domestic product (GDP) by 2037. The current policy challenge is a trade-off between the benefits of beginning to address the long-term debt situation and risking damage to a still fragile economy by engaging in contractionary fiscal policy. In the long term, many argue that debt reduction will eventually become the top priority. Ultimately, debt reduction would require increased tax revenues, reduced government spending, or a combination of the two. If increased tax revenue is part of long-term deficit reduction, expanding the tax base, raising tax rates, or a combination of the two would be required. Income tax rates have been at the center of recent policy debates over taxes. Some have argued that raising tax rates, especially on higher income taxpayers, to increase tax revenues is part of the solution for long-term debt reduction. For example, the Senate recently passed the Middle Class Tax Cut Act (S. 3412), which would allow the 2001 and 2003 Bush tax cuts to expire for taxpayers with income over $250,000 ($200,000 for single taxpayers). Some have argued that higher income tax rates on high income taxpayers would make the overall tax system more progressive. The Senate recently considered legislation, the Paying a Fair Share Act of 2012 (S. 2230), that would implement the "Buffett rule" by raising the tax rate on millionaires. Other recent budget and deficit reduction proposals would reduce tax rates. The President's 2010 Fiscal Commission recommended reducing the budget deficit and tax rates by broadening the tax base—the additional revenues from broadening the tax base would be used for deficit reduction and tax rate reductions. The plan advocated by House Budget Committee Chairman Paul Ryan, the *Path to Prosperity*, also proposes to reduce income tax rates by broadening the tax base. Both plans would broaden the tax base by reducing or eliminating tax expenditures. Advocates of lower tax rates argue that reduced rates would increase economic growth, increase saving and investment, and boost productivity. Proponents of higher tax rates argue that higher tax revenues are necessary for debt reduction, that tax rates on the rich are too low (i.e., they violate the Buffett rule), and that higher tax rates on the rich would moderate increasing income inequality. This report examines individual income tax rates since 1945 in relation to these arguments and seeks to establish what, if any, relationship exists between the top tax rates and economic growth. The nature of these relationships, if any, is explored using statistical analysis. The analysis is limited to the post-World War II period because the U.S. income tax system was not broad-based before the war—less than 15% of families filed a tax return in 1939; 85% filed a return in 1945.

Chapter 2 – This report summarizes the evidence on the relationship between tax rates and economic growth, referring in a number of cases to other CRS reports providing more substance and detail. Potentially negative effects of tax rates on economic growth have been an issue in the debates about whether to extend the 2001-2003 income tax cuts, whether to increase taxes to reduce the deficit, and whether to reform taxes by broadening the base and lowering the rate. Initially, it is important to make a distinction between the effects of policies aimed at short-term stimulation of an underemployed economy and long-run growth. In the short run, both spending increases and tax cuts are projected to increase employment and output in an underemployed economy. These effects operate through the demand side of the economy. In general, the largest effects are from direct government spending and transfers to lower-income individuals, whereas the smallest effects are from cutting taxes of high-income individuals or businesses. Long-run growth is a supply-side phenomenon. In the long run, the availability of jobs is not an issue as an economy naturally creates jobs. Output can grow through increases in labor participation and hours, increases in capital, and changes such as education and technological advances that enhance the productivity of these inputs. Historical data on labor participation rates and average hours worked compared to tax rates indicates little relationship with either top marginal rates or average marginal rates on labor income. Relationships between tax rates and savings appear positively correlated (that is, lower savings are consistent with lower, not higher, tax rates), although this relationship may not be causal. Similarly, during historical periods, slower growth periods have generally been associated with higher, not lower, tax rates. A review of statistical evidence suggests that both labor supply and savings and investment are relatively insensitive to tax rates. Small effects arise in part because of offsetting income and substitution effects (which make the direction of effects uncertain) and in part because each of these individual responses appears small. Institutional constraints may also have an effect. Offsetting income and substitution effects also affect savings. Capital gains taxes are often singled out as determinants of growth, but their effects on the cost of capital are quite small. International capital flows also appear to have a small effect. Most expenditures that affect the productivity of labor and capital inputs (research and development, education, or infrastructure) are already tax favored or provided by the government. Small business taxes are also sometimes emphasized as important to growth, but the evidence suggests a modest and uncertain effect on entrepreneurship. Claims that the cost of tax reductions are significantly reduced by feedback effects do not appear to be justified by the evidence, where feedback effects are in the range of 3% to 10% and can, in some cases, be negative. Because of the estimated realizations response, capital gains tax cuts have in the past been estimated to have a large revenue offset (about 60%), but more recent empirical estimates suggest one of about 20%. In general, for stand-alone rate reductions the additions to the deficit would cause tax cuts to have a larger cost both because of debt service and because of crowding out of investment which would swamp most behavioral effects. This report summarizes the evidence on the relationship between tax rates and economic growth, referring in a number of cases to more-detailed

CRS reports. Potentially negative effects of tax rates on economic growth have been an issue in the debate about whether to extend the 2001-2003 income tax cuts, whether to increase taxes to address the budget deficit, and whether to broaden the base and lower the rates with tax reform. After first distinguishing between short-run counter-cyclical considerations and long-run growth effects, the following section provides some historical data on tax rates and measures of factor supply and growth. This report then reviews the empirical evidence on the major contributors to growth. The final section concludes with a review of dynamic scoring issues.

Chapter 3 – Warren Buffett, the chairman of Berkshire Hathaway, noted that he paid 17.4% of his taxable income in income and payroll taxes—"a lower percentage than was paid by any of the other 20 people" in his office. He stated that "the mega-rich pay income taxes at a rate of 15 percent on most of their earnings but pay practically nothing in payroll taxes." Within a month, the Obama Administration unveiled a plan for economic growth and deficit reduction. The Administration stated that one of its principles for tax reform was to observe the "Buffett rule"—"no household making over $1 million annually should pay a smaller share of its income in taxes than middle-class families pay." In October 2011, Senator Harry Reid introduced the American Jobs Act of 2011 (S. 1660), which contains a 5.6% surtax on millionaires to pay for the provisions of the jobs bill. On March 22, Senator Whitehouse introduced a bill to reduce the deficit by imposing a minimum tax on high-income taxpayers (S. 2230). This report examines the Buffett rule, but uses a measure of income that captures the ability to pay taxes and incorporates the effect of the corporate income tax in addition to the individual income tax and the payroll tax. The results of this analysis show that the current U.S. tax system violates the Buffett rule in that a large proportion of millionaires pay a smaller percentage of their income in taxes than a significant proportion of moderate-income taxpayers. Roughly a quarter of all millionaires (about 94,500 taxpayers) face a tax rate that is lower than the tax rate faced by 10.4 million moderate-income taxpayers (10% of the moderate-income taxpayers). Tax reforms that are consistent with the Buffett rule would likely include raising tax rates on capital gains and dividends. For example, the President has proposed allowing the 2001 and 2003 Bush tax cuts to expire for high-income taxpayers and taxing carried interests of hedge fund managers as ordinary income as tax reforms that observe the Buffett rule. Research suggests that these tax reforms are unlikely to affect many small businesses or to deter saving and investment. In August 2011, Warren Buffett, the chairman of Berkshire Hathaway, published an opinion piece in the *New York Times*. He noted that he paid 17.4% of his taxable income in income and payroll taxes—"a lower percentage than was paid by any of the other 20 people" in his office. He stated that "the mega-rich pay income taxes at a rate of 15 percent on most of their earnings but pay practically nothing in payroll taxes." He proposed that tax rates be raised for taxpayers making more than $1 million. One month later, the Obama Administration unveiled a plan for economic growth and deficit reduction. The Administration stated that one of its principles for tax reform was to observe the "Buffett rule"—"no household making over $1 million annually should pay a smaller share of its income in taxes than middle-class families pay." The reaction to the Buffett rule tax reform principle was swift, with some accusing the President of engaging in class-warfare. In October 2011, Senator Harry Reid introduced the American Jobs Act of 2011 (S. 1660), which contains a 5.6% surtax on millionaires to pay for the provisions of the jobs bill. On March 22, Senator Whitehouse introduced a bill to reduce the deficit by imposing a minimum tax on high-income taxpayers (S. 2230). This report examines the validity of the Buffett rule and the issues surrounding the rule.

Chapter 4 – A series of tax cuts were enacted early in the George W. Bush Administration by the Economic Growth and Tax Relief Reconciliation Act of 2001 (EGTRRA) and the Jobs and Growth Tax Relief Reconciliation Act of 2003 (JGTRRA). These tax cuts, which are collectively known as the Bush tax cuts, were originally scheduled to expire at the end of 2010. These tax provisions were extended until the end of 2012 at an estimated cost of $408 billion. Beginning in 2013, many of the individual income tax parameters (such as tax rates) will revert back to 2000 levels. One legislative proposal introduced in the 112th Congress, H.R. 6104 (introduced by Representative Cedric Richmond), would extend the 2001, 2003, and 2009 tax cuts for taxpayers with income below $500,000 for another year. A proposal by Senator Harry Reid (S. 3393) would extend the tax cuts for taxpayers with income below $200,000 (for singles) or $250,000 (for married couples) for another year, but set a top income tax rate on qualified dividends of 20%. The 2010 debate over the fate of the Bush tax cuts took place when the economy was underperforming, the unemployment rate was high, and the federal deficit was large. The U.S. economy was in a severe recession from December 2007 to June 2009. The unemployment rate reached a high of 10.2% in October 2009, and it is currently still over 8%. As a result of reduced economic activity and government efforts to stimulate the economy, the federal budget deficit increased from 1.2% of GDP in FY2007 to 9.9% of GDP in FY2009. Most economic forecasts suggest the economic and budget outlook will likely be characterized by high unemployment, sluggish economic growth, and relatively large budget deficits. Consequently, the 2012 debate over the fate of the Bush tax cuts is also likely to take place in a bleak economic and fiscal environment. There are several options that Congress may consider regarding the Bush tax cuts, and each of the options strikes a different balance between fostering economic growth and restoring fiscal sustainability. Allowing the Bush tax cuts to expire as scheduled will somewhat improve the fiscal condition by increasing tax revenue, but could retard the economic recovery. At the other extreme, permanently extending all of the Bush tax cuts would not undercut the economic recovery, but would somewhat worsen the longer-term fiscal outlook and possibly signal a lack of progress in dealing with the long-term fiscal situation. Permanently extending the Bush tax cuts could increase federal debt by almost $3 trillion over the next 10 years. It is often argued that increasing tax rates will reduce consumer spending in the short term, and work effort, saving and investment—all key components of economic growth—in the long term. In an underemployed economy, short-term spending increases and tax cuts are expected to facilitate job creation, reduce unemployment, and increase output. The main argument against allowing the Bush tax cuts to expire at the end of 2010 was the weak recovery and the fear of pushing the economy back into recession, an argument likely to be made in 2012. Once the economy has recovered from the recession, however, long-term economic growth will be facilitated by increasing work effort, saving, and investment. It is often argued that increasing tax rates will reduce these long-term economic growth components. Economic research, however, suggests that modest tax rate increases would have little negative impact on long-term economic growth and job creation. A series of tax cuts were enacted early in the George W. Bush Administration by the Economic Growth and Tax Relief Reconciliation Act of 2001 (EGTRRA; P.L. 107-16) and the Jobs and Growth Tax Relief Reconciliation Act of 2003 (JGTRRA; P.L. 108-27). These tax cuts, which are collectively known as the Bush tax cuts, were originally scheduled to expire at the end of 2010. In addition to the Bush tax cuts, two tax provisions enacted in the American Recovery and Reinvestment Act of 2009 (ARRA; P.L. 111-5)—an increase in the earned income tax credit and an increase in eligibility for the refundable portion of the child tax credit—were scheduled to expire at the end of 2010. In a lame-duck session in December 2010, the Bush tax cuts and the two ARRA provisions were extended for two years at an estimated cost of $408 billion.[1] Beginning in 2013, many of the individual income tax parameters (such as tax rates) are scheduled to revert back to 2000 levels. One legislative proposal introduced in the 112th Congress, H.R. 6104 (introduced by Representative Cedric Richmond), would extend the 2001, 2003 and 2009 tax cuts for taxpayers with income below $500,000 for another year. A proposal by Senator Harry Reid (S. 3393) would extend the tax cuts for taxpayers with income below $200,000 (for singles) or $250,000 (for married couples) for another year, but set a top income tax rate on qualified dividends of 20%. The pending expiration of the Bush tax cuts generated a great deal of attention in 2010 as reflected by editorials and opinion pieces in national newspapers, and congressional hearings. The proposals regarding the Bush tax cuts were generally not about whether to let the tax cuts expire as scheduled, but rather about which tax cuts to extend and for how long. Many policy makers argued that raising taxes could impede the fragile economic recovery from the severe 2007-2009 recession. The major tax provisions in EGTRRA and JGTRRA and the tax provisions in ARRA that are part of the current debate over the Bush tax cuts are the reduced individual income tax rates, the reduction of the marriage penalty (and increase in the marriage bonus), the repeal of the personal exemption phaseout and the limitation on itemized deductions, the reduced tax rates on long-term capital gains and qualified dividends, and expanded tax credits. Other provisions that were included in EGTRRA and JGTRRA, such as the estate tax, are not considered in this study. This report examines the Bush tax cuts within the context of the current and long-term economic and budgetary environment.

Chapter 5 – One provision of the 1913 individual income tax that generated a great deal of confusion was the taxation of income from the sale of property (i.e., capital gains income). This initial confusion has led to almost 100 years of legislative debates over capital gains. Beginning in 1922 capital gains were first subject to lower tax rates than ordinary income. This preferential treatment has continued throughout most of the history of the income tax. Proposals dealing with the taxation of capital gains have ranged from the outright elimination of capital gains taxation to the reduction of capital gains tax rates for certain classes of taxpayers to the elimination of the preferential tax treatment. Overall, capital gains tax revenues have been a fairly small, but not trivial, source of government revenue. Since 1954, revenue from the capital gains tax as a share of total income tax revenue has averaged 5.2%. It reached a peak of 12.8% in 1986 and a low of 2.0% in 1957. Nonetheless, the 2007 capital gains tax revenue of $123 billion was equal to 75% of the FY2007 budget deficit. Some argue that reducing capital gains tax rates will increase tax revenues by dramatically increasing capital gains realizations. While the effect of changes in the capital gains tax rate continue to be debated and researched, the bulk of the evidence suggests that reducing the capital gains tax rate reduces tax revenues. Higher income households are substantially more likely to own assets that can generate taxable gains than lower income households. Additionally, high income households own most of these assets, realize most of the capital gains, and pay most of the capital gains taxes at preferential rates. Capital gains tax reductions are often proposed as a policy that will increase saving and investment, provide a short-term economic stimulus, and boost long-term economic growth. Capital gains tax rate reductions appear to decrease public saving and may have little or no effect on private saving. Consequently, many analysts note that capital gains tax reductions likely have a negative overall impact on national saving. Furthermore, capital gains tax rate reductions, they observe, are unlikely to have much effect on the long-term level of output or the path to the long-run level of output (i.e., economic growth). A tax reduction on capital gains would mostly benefit very high income taxpayers who are likely to save most of any tax reduction. A temporary capital gains tax reduction possibly could have a negative impact on short-term economic growth.

In: Tax Rates
Editor: Howard P. Durham
ISBN: 978-1-62417-215-1

Chapter 1

TAXES AND THE ECONOMY: AN ECONOMIC ANALYSIS OF THE TOP TAX RATES SINCE 1945*

Thomas L. Hungerford

SUMMARY

Income tax rates have been at the center of recent policy debates over taxes. Some policymakers have argued that raising tax rates, especially on higher income taxpayers, to increase tax revenues is part of the solution for long-term debt reduction. For example, the Senate recently passed the Middle Class Tax Cut (S. 3412), which would allow the 2001 and 2003 Bush tax cuts to expire for taxpayers with income over $250,000 ($200,000 for single taxpayers). The Senate recently considered legislation, the Paying a Fair Share Act of 2012 (S. 2230), that would implement the "Buffett rule" by raising the tax rate on millionaires.

Other recent budget and deficit reduction proposals would reduce tax rates. The President's 2010 Fiscal Commission recommended reducing the budget deficit and tax rates by broadening the tax base—the additional revenues from broadening the tax base would be used for deficit reduction and tax rate reductions. The plan advocated by House Budget Committee

* This is an edited, reformatted and augmented version of the Congressional Research Service Publication, CRS Report for Congress R42729, dated September 14, 2012.

Chairman Paul Ryan that is embodied in the House Budget Resolution (H.Con.Res. 112), the *Path to Prosperity*, also proposes to reduce income tax rates by broadening the tax base. Both plans would broaden the tax base by reducing or eliminating tax expenditures.

Advocates of lower tax rates argue that reduced rates would increase economic growth, increase saving and investment, and boost productivity (increase the economic pie). Proponents of higher tax rates argue that higher tax revenues are necessary for debt reduction, that tax rates on the rich are too low (i.e., they violate the Buffett rule), and that higher tax rates on the rich would moderate increasing income inequality (change how the economic pie is distributed). This report attempts to clarify whether or not there is an association between the tax rates of the highest income taxpayers and economic growth. Data is analyzed to illustrate the association between the tax rates of the highest income taxpayers and measures of economic growth.

Throughout the late-1940s and 1950s, the top marginal tax rate was typically above 90%; today it is 35%. Additionally, the top capital gains tax rate was 25% in the 1950s and 1960s, 35% in the 1970s; today it is 15%. The real GDP growth rate averaged 4.2% and real per capita GDP increased annually by 2.4% in the 1950s. In the 2000s, the average real GDP growth rate was 1.7% and real per capita GDP increased annually by less than 1%. There is not conclusive evidence, however, to substantiate a clear relationship between the 65-year steady reduction in the top tax rates and economic growth. Analysis of such data suggests the reduction in the top tax rates have had little association with saving, investment, or productivity growth. However, the top tax rate reductions appear to be associated with the increasing concentration of income at the top of the income distribution. The share of income accruing to the top 0.1% of U.S. families increased from 4.2% in 1945 to 12.3% by 2007 before falling to 9.2% due to the 2007-2009 recession. The evidence does not suggest necessarily a relationship between tax policy with regard to the top tax rates and the size of the economic pie, but there may be a relationship to how the economic pie is sliced.

The U.S. unemployment rate has been over 8% since February 2009 and the Blue Chip consensus forecast has it remaining above 8% throughout 2012. In addition, if current fiscal policies continue, the United States could be facing a debt level approaching 200% of gross domestic product (GDP) by 2037.[1] The current policy challenge is a trade-off between the benefits of beginning to address the long-term debt situation and risking damage to a still fragile economy by engaging in contractionary fiscal policy.[2] In the long term, many argue that debt reduction will eventually become the top priority.

Ultimately, debt reduction would require increased tax revenues, reduced government spending, or a combination of the two. If increased tax revenue is part of long-term deficit reduction, expanding the tax base, raising tax rates, or a combination of the two would be required.

Income tax rates have been at the center of recent policy debates over taxes. Some have argued that raising tax rates, especially on higher income taxpayers, to increase tax revenues is part of the solution for long-term debt reduction. For example, the Senate recently passed the Middle Class Tax Cut Act (S. 3412), which would allow the 2001 and 2003 Bush tax cuts to expire for taxpayers with income over $250,000 ($200,000 for single taxpayers).[3] Some have argued that higher income tax rates on high income taxpayers would make the overall tax system more progressive.[4] The Senate recently considered legislation, the Paying a Fair Share Act of 2012 (S. 2230), that would implement the "Buffett rule" by raising the tax rate on millionaires.[5]

Other recent budget and deficit reduction proposals would reduce tax rates. The President's 2010 Fiscal Commission recommended reducing the budget deficit and tax rates by broadening the tax base—the additional revenues from broadening the tax base would be used for deficit reduction and tax rate reductions.[6] The plan advocated by House Budget Committee Chairman Paul Ryan, the *Path to Prosperity*, also proposes to reduce income tax rates by broadening the tax base. Both plans would broaden the tax base by reducing or eliminating tax expenditures.[7]

Advocates of lower tax rates argue that reduced rates would increase economic growth, increase saving and investment, and boost productivity. Proponents of higher tax rates argue that higher tax revenues are necessary for debt reduction, that tax rates on the rich are too low (i.e., they violate the Buffett rule), and that higher tax rates on the rich would moderate increasing income inequality. This report examines individual income tax rates since 1945 in relation to these arguments and seeks to establish what, if any, relationship exists between the top tax rates and economic growth. The nature of these relationships, if any, is explored using statistical analysis. The analysis is limited to the post-World War II period because the U.S. income tax system was not broad-based before the war—less than 15% of families filed a tax return in 1939; 85% filed a return in 1945.

Top Tax Rates Since 1945

Tax policy analysts often use two concepts of tax rates. The first is the marginal tax rate or the tax rate on the last dollar of income. If a taxpayer's income were to increase by $1, the marginal tax rate indicates what proportion of that dollar would be paid in taxes. The highest marginal tax rate is referred to as the top marginal tax rate. How much an additional dollar is taxed depends on if it is ordinary income (e.g., wages) or capital gains. The second concept of tax rates is the average tax rate, which is the proportion of all income that is paid in taxes. An examination of the trend in the average tax rate provides information on how the tax burden has changed over time.

Although the statutory top marginal tax rate was over 90% in the 1950s, the average tax rate for the very rich was much lower. The average tax rates at five-year intervals since 1945 for the top 0.1% and top 0.01% of taxpayers is shown in **Figure 1**. The average tax rate for the top 0.01% (one taxpayer in 10,000) was about 60% in 1945 and fell to 24.2% by 1990. The average tax rate for the top 0.1% (one taxpayer in 1,000) was 55% in 1945 and also fell to 24.2% by 1990, following a similar downward path as the tax rate for the top 0.01%. Between 1990 and 1995, the average tax rate for both the top 0.1% and top 0.01% increased to about 31%. After 1995, the average tax rate for the top 0.01% was lower than that for the top 0.1%.

The trends in the statutory top marginal tax rate and the top capital gains tax rate are displayed in **Figure 2**. The general trend for the top marginal tax rate has been downward since 1945 (the higher, solid line in the figure). It fell from 94% in 1945 to 91% in the 1950s and 70% in the 1960s and 1970s to a low of 28% after the enactment of the Tax Reform Act of 1986 (TRA86; P.L. 99-514).[8] The top marginal tax rate subsequently increased to 39.6% in the 1990s, before being reduced to its current level of 35% by the Economic Growth and Tax Relief Reconciliation Act of 2001 (EGTRRA; P.L. 107-16).

The variation in the top capital gains tax rate since 1945 has been much lower and there appears to be no distinctive trend (the lower, dashed line). The top capital gains tax rate was 25% before 1965, was raised to 35% in the 1970s, fell to 20% in the early 1980s, and rose to 28% after the enactment of TRA86. The rate was reduced to its current level of 15% (from 20%) by the Jobs and Growth Tax Relief Reconciliation Act of 2003 (JGTRRA; P.L. 108-27). The top capital gains tax rate is scheduled to return to 20% at the end of 2012.

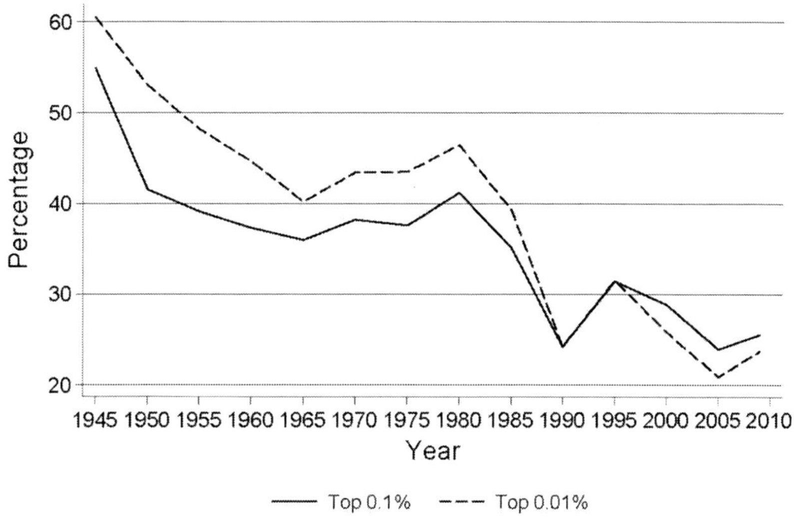

Source: CRS calculations using Internal Revenue Service (IRS) Statistics of Income (SOI) information.

Note: The vertical axis is the average tax rate.

Figure 1. Average Tax Rates for the Highest-Income Taxpayers, 1945-2009.

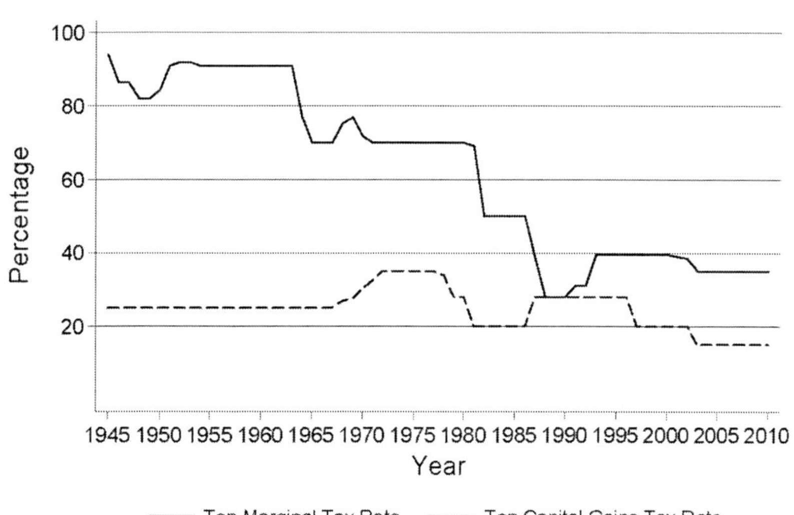

Source: Internal Revenue Service.

Figure 2. Top Marginal Tax Rate and Top Capital Gains Tax Rate, 1945-2010.

Top Tax Rates and the Economy

Some economists and policymakers often assert that reducing marginal tax rates would spur economic growth.[9] This could work through several mechanisms. First, lower tax rates could give people more after-tax income that could be used to purchase additional goods and services. This is a demand-side argument and is often invoked to support a temporary tax reduction as an expansionary fiscal stimulus. Second, reduced tax rates could boost saving and investment, which would increase the productive capacity of the economy and productivity.[10] Furthermore, some argue that reduced tax rates increase labor supply by increasing the after-tax wage rate. There is substantial evidence, however, to suggest that labor supply responses to wage and tax changes are small for both men and women.[11] To the extent that these mechanisms are valid, it is expected that there would be an inverse relationship between the top tax rates and saving, investment, productivity growth, and real per capita GDP growth. Each relationship is examined.

Saving and Investment

Analysts caution against a low saving rate. They argue that high capital investment leads to higher economic growth and a higher future standard of living. But if capital investment is not financed by national saving it has to be financed by borrowing abroad.[12] Persistent borrowing from abroad builds up international liabilities and implies increasing flow of funds will be sent abroad as interest and dividends.

National saving is composed of two components: private saving and public saving. Private saving is the saving by households and businesses while public saving is the budget surpluses of local, state, and federal governments. If spending is greater than income, then saving is negative (i.e., people are reducing wealth or borrowing).

From an economic perspective, the effect of taxes on private saving is ambiguous. If taxes are reduced, the after-tax return on saving is larger; consequently, individuals may be able to maintain a target level of wealth and save less (wealth will grow due to the higher after-tax returns). This is the income effect and has lower taxes leading to less saving. However, the reduced after-tax return changes the relative price of consuming now (saving less) and future consumption (saving more) in favor of future consumption. This is the substitution effect and has lower taxes leading to more saving. The actual effect of a tax reduction depends on the relative magnitudes of the income and substitution effects.[13]

The simple relationships between the private saving ratio and the top tax rates are displayed in the top two charts in **Figure 3**.[14] Each point represents the private saving ratio and top tax rate for each year since 1945. The nature of the relationship is illustrated by the straight line in the figure, which graphically represents the correlation (fitted relationship or fitted values) between the two variables.[15] The slope of the fitted values line indicates how one variable changes when the other variable changes. For both the top marginal tax rate and the top capital gains tax rate there seems to be a positive relationship—the higher the tax rate, the higher the saving ratio. The observed correlation between the tax rates and the saving ratio, however, could be coincidental or spurious. Estimation of the correlations controlling for other factors affecting saving and paying particular attention to the statistical properties of the variables indicates that the relationship observed in **Figure 3** is likely coincidental (and not statistically significant)—suggesting the top tax rates are not associated with private saving.[16] Other research suggests that taxes generally have had a negligible effect on private saving.[17] But public saving can be reduced if tax revenue is reduced due to tax rate reductions. The overall effect of tax reductions on national saving could be negative—that is, national saving falls.[18]

Taxes can affect investment not only through the income and substitution effects related to saving, but also through a risk-taking effect. The capital gains tax rate has been singled out as being important to investment. For risk-averse investors, the capital gains tax could act as insurance for risky investments by reducing the losses as well as the gains—it decreases the variability of investment returns.[19] Consequently, a rise in the capital gains top rate could increase investment because of reduced risk.

The bottom charts in **Figure 3** show the observed relation between the private fixed investment ratio (investment divided by potential GDP) and the top tax rates. The fitted values suggest there is a negative relationship between the investment ratio and top tax rates. But regression analysis does not find the correlations to be statistically significant (see **Table A-1** in the appendix) suggesting that the top tax rates do not necessarily have a demonstrably significant relationship with investment.[20]

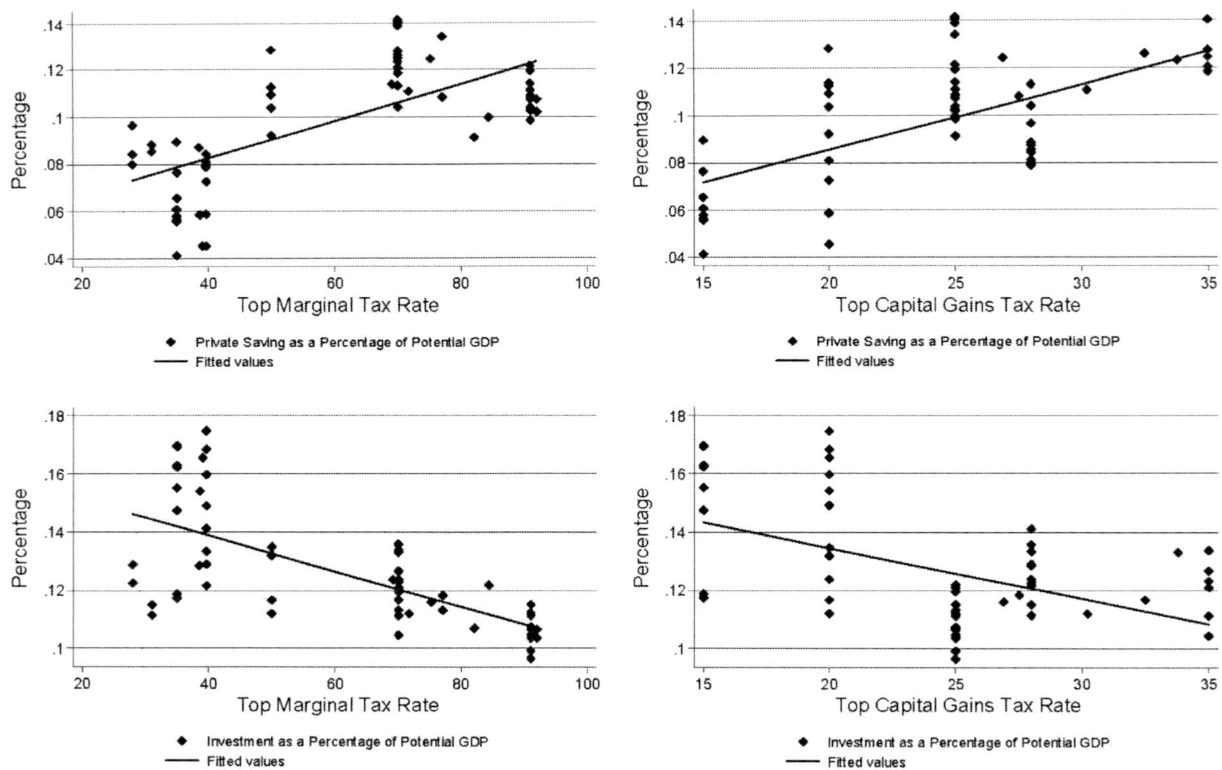

Source: CRS analysis.

Figure 3. Private Saving, Investment, and the Top Tax Rates, 1945-2010.

Productivity Growth

Productivity can increase due to investment, innovation, improvement in labor skills, increases in entrepreneurship, and enhanced competition.[21] It is often argued that lower tax rates have a positive effect on all of these factors. Consequently, it would be expected that lower tax rates enhance productivity growth. **Figure 4** displays the relationship between labor productivity growth and the top tax rates. The fitted values suggest that the top marginal tax rate has a slight positive association with productivity growth while the top capital gains tax rate has a slight negative association with productivity growth. The regression analysis, however, does not find either relationship to be statistically significant (see **Table A-1**), suggesting the top tax rates are not necessarily associated with productivity growth.

Real Per Capita GDP Growth

The annual real per capita GDP growth rate plotted against the top marginal tax rate and top capital gains tax rate is shown in **Figure 5**. Each point represents the real per capita GDP growth rate and tax rate for each year since 1945. The fitted values seem to suggest that higher tax rates are associated with slightly higher real per capita GDP growth rates. The top marginal tax rate in the 1950s was over 90%, and the real GDP growth rate averaged 4.2% and real per capita GDP increased annually by 2.4% in the 1950s. In the 2000s, the top marginal tax rate was 35% while the average real GDP growth rate was 1.7% and real per capita GDP increased annually by less than 1%.

The scattered points, however, generally are not close to the fitted values line indicating that the association between GDP growth and the top tax rates is not strong.[22] Furthermore, the observed positive association between real GDP growth and the top tax rates shown in the figure could be coincidental or spurious because of changes to the U.S. economy over the past 65 years.[23] The statistical analysis using multivariate regression (reported in **Table A-1**) does not find that either top tax rate has a statistically significant association with the real GDP growth rate.[24]

These results are generally consistent with previous research on tax cuts. Some studies find that a broad based tax rate reduction has a small to modest, positive effect on economic growth.[25] Other studies have found that a broad based tax reduction, such as the Bush tax cuts, has no effect on economic growth.[26] It would be reasonable to assume that a tax rate change limited to a small group of taxpayers at the top of the income distribution would have a negligible effect on economic growth.

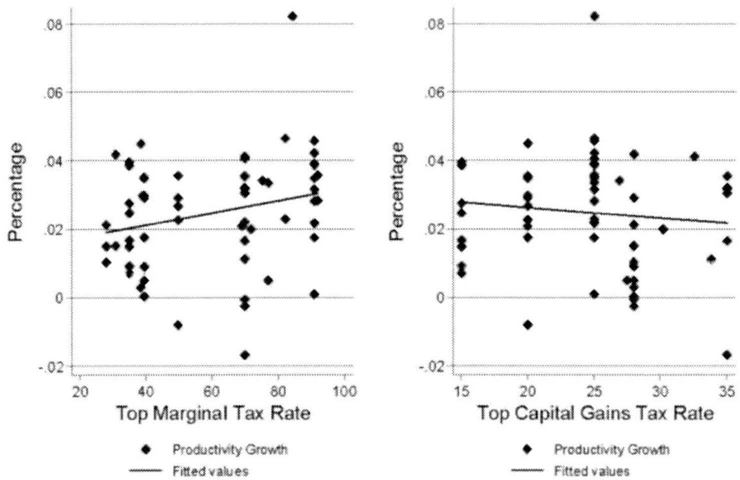

Source: CRS analysis.
Note: The vertical axis is the labor productivity growth rate.

Figure 4. Labor Productivity Growth Rates and the Top Tax Rates, 1945-2010.

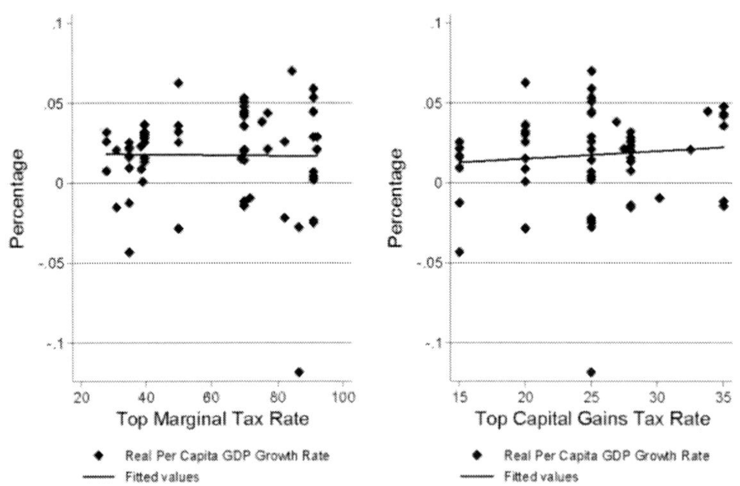

Source: CRS analysis.
Note: The vertical axis is the real per capita GDP growth rate.

Figure 5. Real Per Capita GDP Growth Rate and the Top Tax Rates, 1945-2010.

TOP TAX RATES AND THE DISTRIBUTION OF INCOME

It is recognized that measure of U.S. income disparities have increased over the past 35 years.[27] According to income tax data, average inflation-adjusted or real income increased by 116% (that is, about doubled) since 1945.[28] Average real income increased by 395% for the top 0.1% and by 692% for the top 0.01% over this period. Average real income for the balance of the top 1% in the income distribution (i.e., all but the top 0.1%) increased by about 165%. The share of income going to the top 1% increased from 12.5% in 1945 to 19.8% in 2010. Three-quarters of this increase in income share went to the top 0.1%. Since the major changes in the distribution of income were largely due to changes in the top 0.1% of the income distribution, the focus of the analysis is on the top 0.1%.

Arguments are offered for and against reducing income inequality. The classic argument against rising income inequality is the rich get richer and the poor get poorer. This can increase poverty, reduce well-being, and reduce social cohesion. Consequently, many argue that reducing income inequality may reduce various social ills. Some researchers are concerned about the consequences of rising income inequality. Some research has found that large income and class disparities adversely affect health and economic well-being.[29]

In contrast, others point out that average real income has been rising, so while the rich are getting richer, the poor are not necessarily getting poorer. In addition, many argue that some income inequality is necessary to encourage innovation and entrepreneurship—the possibility of large rewards and high income are incentives to bear the risks.[30] Many argue that income or social mobility reduces income inequality and increases well-being.[31]

Figure 6 displays the trend in the income (before taxes) share of the top 0.1% (the top solid line in the figure) and the top 0.01% (the lower dashed line) since 1945.[32] Under both definitions of the top of the income distribution (i.e., the rich), the income shares were relatively stable until the late 1970s and then started to rise. In 1945, the income share of the top 0.1% was 4.2%, increased to 12.3% by 2007, fell during the 2007-2009 recession, and started to rise again in 2010.[33] The income share of the top 0.01% followed the same overall trend.

The observed relationship between the top tax rates and the income share of the top 0.1% and the top 0.1% are displayed in **Figure 7** (the top 0.1%) and **Figure 8** (the top 0.01%). Under both definitions of the rich, the fitted values suggest that there is a strong negative relationship between the top tax rates and the income shares accruing to families at the top of the income distribution. These results suggest that as the top tax rates are reduced, the share of income accruing to the top of the income distribution increases—that is, income disparities increase. The regression analysis results reported in **Table A-2** show that these relationships are statistically significant. Similar results by other researchers have been obtained for other countries.[34]

Source: Piketty and Saez.
Note: The vertical axis is the share of total income.

Figure 6. Shares of Total Income of the Top 0.1% and Top 0.01% Since 1945.

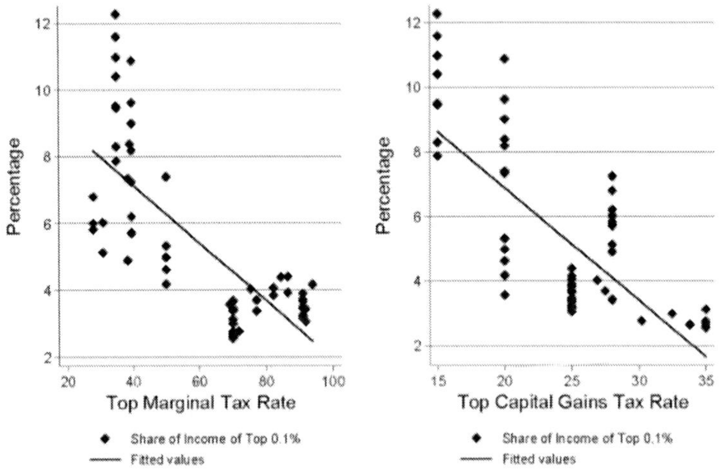

Source: CRS analysis of Piketty and Saez data.
Note: The vertical axis is the share of total income.

Figure 7. Share of Total Income of Top 0.1% and the Top Tax Rates, 1945-2010.

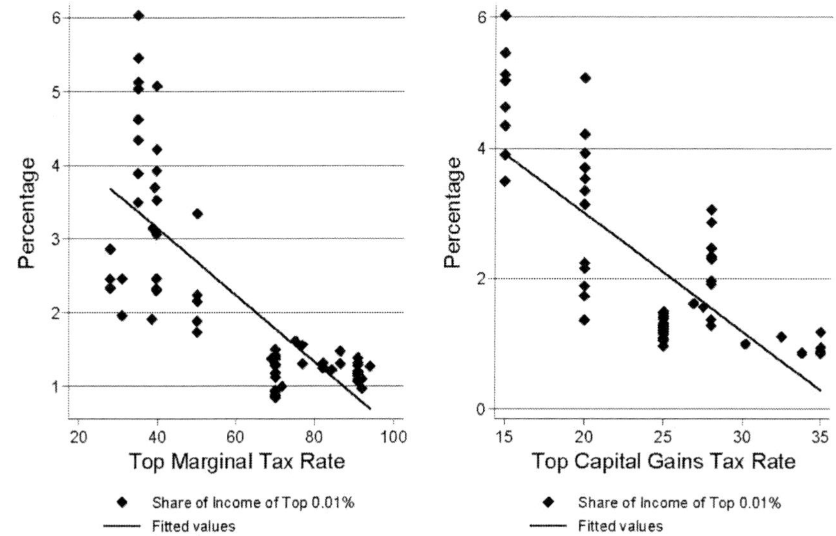

Source: CRS analysis of Piketty and Saez data.

Note: The vertical axis is the share of total income.

Figure 8. Share of Total Income of Top 0.01% and the Top Tax Rates, 1945-2010.

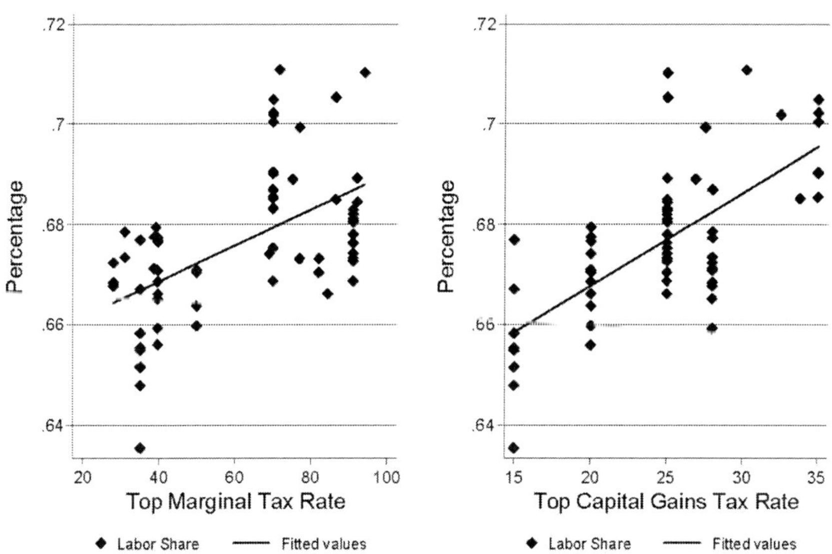

Source: CRS analysis.

Note: The vertical axis is the share of national income accruing to labor.

Figure 9. Labor Share of Income and the Top Tax Rates, 1945-2010.

Research has shown that changes in capital gains and dividends were the largest contributor to the increase in income inequality since the mid-1990s.[35] Capital gains and dividends have become a larger share of total income over the past decade and a half while earnings have become a smaller share.[36] This suggests that labor's share of income could also be related to the top tax rates.[37] **Figure 9** displays this relationship. The fitted values show that the labor share of income is higher with higher top marginal tax rates and higher top capital gains tax rates. This relationship is statistically significant (see **Table A-2**).

Tax policy affects after-tax income. Since the U.S. individual income tax is a progressive tax system, after-tax incomes tend to be more equally distributed than before-tax income.[38] Changes in tax policy would change the distribution of after-tax income. Research has demonstrated that tax policy has a less equalizing effect now than it did in the mid-1990s and in 1979.[39]

The results suggest that pre-tax incomes tend to be more equally distributed and labor's share of income larger when the top tax rates are higher. Two related explanations have been offered that are consistent with these results. Jacob Hacker and Paul Pierson argue that some public policies benefit the few high-income families rather than middle- and low-income families.[40] In a related explanation, Thomas Piketty, Emmanuel Saez, and Stefanie Stantcheva argue that high top tax rates were part of the institutional structure that restrained top income by reducing gains from bargaining or rent extraction by CEOs and managers.[41] For example, a CEO has less incentive to bargain hard over additional compensation when he keeps 9 cents of every additional dollar (a 91% top tax rate) than when he keeps 65 cents of every additional dollar (a 35% top tax rate). A recent study by Jon Bakija, Adam Cole, and Bradley Heim provides additional support for this mechanism—60% of taxpayers in the top 0.1% are in occupations that provide some bargaining power over compensation (executives, managers, supervisors, and financial professions).[42]

CONCLUDING REMARKS

The top income tax rates have changed considerably since the end of World War II. Throughout the late-1940s and 1950s, the top marginal tax rate was typically above 90%; today it is 35%. Additionally, the top capital gains tax rate was 25% in the 1950s and 1960s, 35% in the 1970s; today it is 15%. The average tax rate faced by the top 0.01% of taxpayers was above 40% until the mid-1980s; today it is below 25%. Tax rates affecting taxpayers at the top of the income distribution are currently at their lowest levels since the end of the second World War.

The results of the analysis suggest that changes over the past 65 years in the top marginal tax rate and the top capital gains tax rate do not appear correlated with economic growth. The reduction in the top tax rates appears to be uncorrelated with saving, investment, and productivity growth. The top tax rates appear to have little or no relation to the size of the economic pie.

However, the top tax rate reductions appear to be associated with the increasing concentration of income at the top of the income distribution. As measured by IRS data, the share of income accruing to the top 0.1% of U.S. families increased from 4.2% in 1945 to 12.3% by 2007 before falling to 9.2% due to the 2007-2009 recession. At the same time, the average tax rate paid by the top 0.1% fell from over 50% in 1945 to about 25% in 2009. Tax policy could have a relation to how the economic pie is sliced—lower top tax rates may be associated with greater income disparities.

APPENDIX. DATA AND SUPPLEMENTAL ANALYSIS

For the analysis, data was gathered from a variety of publicly available sources:

- Top marginal tax rates and top capital gains tax rates: IRS, Statistics of Income, various tables available at http://www.irs.gov/taxstats/indtaxstats/0,,id=98123,00.html.
- Real per capita GDP, private saving, real private fixed investment, income tax revenue, real federal current expenditures, real federal transfers, disposable personal income, population: Dept. of Commerce, Bureau of Economic Analysis, National Income and Product Account tables, various tables available at http://www.bea.gov/iTable/index_nipa.cfm.
- Labor share of income: calculated from National Income and Product Account tables, various tables using method of José-Víctor Ríos-Rull and Raul Santaeulalia-Llopis, "Redistributive Shocks and Productivity Shocks," *Journal of Monetary Economics*, vol. 57, no. 8 (November 2010), pp. 931-948.
- Labor productivity: Dept. of Labor, Bureau of Labor Statistics, available at http://www.bls.gov/lpc/.

- Income shares of top 0.1% and top 0.01%: Thomas Piketty and Emmanuel Saez, "Income Inequality in the United States, 1913-1998," *Quarterly Journal of Economics*, vol. 118, no. 1 (February 2003), pp. 1-39, with updated tables available at http://elsa.berkeley.edu/~saez/.
- Potential GDP: CBO, available at http://www.cbo.gov/publication/42912.
- SandP annual stock returns, real home price index: Robert Shiller, Yale University, available at http://www.econ.yale.edu/~shiller/data.htm.
- AAA Bond yield: St. Louis Federal Reserve Bank, available at http://research.stlouisfed.org/fred2/categories/119.
- College graduates: Census Bureau, available at http://www.census.gov/hhes/socdemo/education/data/cps/historical/index.html.

Multivariate time-series regression techniques were used to determine the statistical significance of the estimated relation between the top tax rates and the various indicators of economic growth. The standard errors were corrected allowing for heteroskedastic and autocorrelated error-term using the Newey-West procedure with 5 lags. All variables were tested for the presence of a unit root. Most variables were found to have a unit root; these variable were first differenced for the analysis (i.e., the one year change in the variable is used in the analysis). The other explanatory variables included in the analyses have been used by other researchers.

The right-hand side variables of interest are the statutory top tax rates for ordinary income and capital gains. The top marginal tax rate is denoted by MTR and the top capital gains tax rates is denoted by KTR. The top tax rate variables are entered into the regressions as the after-tax or net-of-tax shares, which are equal to 1 minus the top tax rates (1-MTR and 1-KTR). Consequently, a negative coefficient estimate indicates a positive relationship between the top tax rate and the indicator of economic growth. The regression results are reported in **Table A-1**.

The four regression equations are:

- *Saving ratio and investment ratio*. Private saving and private fixed investment are expressed as a percentage of potential GDP (the level of GDP attainable when resources are fully employed). In addition to the tax variables, other right-hand side variables in both regressions include the SandP stock return and the AAA corporate bond return. The percentage change in the house price index and the growth rate of disposable personal income are included in the saving ratio regression.[43] The investment ratio regression also includes the 1-year lagged change in investment ratio as a right-hand side variable, which represents "investment inertia."[44]

Table A-1. Regression Results: Economic Growth Standard Errors in Parentheses

	Change in Private Saving Ratio	Change in Private Fixed Investment Ratio	Change in Labor Productivity Growth Rate	Real Per Capita GDP Growth Rate
Constant	-0.0025	-0.0002	-0.0044	0.0219
Δ(1-MTR)	0.0442 (0.0366)	-0.0079 (0.0280)	-0.0139 (0.0633)	-0.0992 (0.1026)
Δ(1-KTR)	0.0277 (0.0341)	0.0334 (0.0241)	0.1119 (0.0697)	-0.0369 (0.0661)
Log of Disposable Personal Income	0.0325 (0.0759)			
ΔAAA Bond Rate	0.0357 (0.0603)	-0.0053 (0.0968)		
SandP Stock Return	0.0035 (0.0097)	0.0033 (0.0058)		
Percent Change in Real Home Price Index	-0.0485 (0.0295)			
1-year lag of Change in Private Fixed Investment Ratio		0.2652*** (0.0979)		
ΔCollege Graduates as Percent of Population			0.4952 (0.8292)	-0.2650 (0.7916)
ΔReal Federal Transfers Ratio			1.6150*** (0.2767)	
ΔPopulation Growth Rate				-5.9978 (3.6830)
ΔReal Federal Current Expenditures Ratio				-0.6445 (0.5753)
F-statistic	1.02	2.47	9.12	1.14

Source: CRS analysis.

Note: Δ - indicates the 1-year change in the variable; *** statistically significant at 1% level.

- *Productivity growth.* Labor productivity is an index of output per hour; it can be affected not only by taxes but also by the quantity and quality of the labor force. The indicators of the quantity and quality of the labor force include the change in the proportion of the population in their prime-age working years (25 to 64 years), the change in the proportion of the population with at least a 4-year college degree, and the change in federal transfer payments (as a percentage of potential GDP) to capture work disincentive effects of government programs.
- *Real per capita GDP growth.* In addition to the tax rate variables, right-hand side variables include the population growth rate, the change in the proportion of the population with at least a 4-year college degree, and the change in federal current expenditures as a percentage of potential GDP.[45]

Table A-2. Regression Results: Income Inequality Standard Errors in Parentheses

	Change in Log Top 0.1% Share	Change in Log Top 0.01% Share	Change in Labor Share
Constant	0.0068	0.0073	-0.0055
Δ(1-MTR)	0.6241* (0.3601)	0.4756* (0.2483)	-0.0168* (0.0084)
Δ(1-KTR)	3.7512*** (1.3076)	2.5991*** (0.9598)	-0.0510** (0.0198)
Lagged Real GDP Growth	0.0006 (0.0046)	-0.0010 (0.0040)	0.0016*** (0.0001)
F-statistic	3.52	3.30	42.77

Source: CRS analysis.

Note: Δ - indicates the 1-year change in the variable; *** statistically significant at 1% level; ** statistically significant at 5% level; * statistically significant at 10% level.

The results reported in **Table A-1** suggest that neither the top marginal tax rate nor the top capital gains tax rate are strongly correlated with saving, investment, labor productivity, and GDP growth controlling for other covariates.

Time-series regression techniques were also used to determine the statistical significance of the correlation between the top tax rates and the measures of income shares. The income shares of the top 0.1% and top 0.01% were converted to logarithms. In addition, following the specifications of other researchers, the 1-year lagged real GDP growth rate was included as an explanatory variable.[46] The results are reported in **Table A-2**.

End Notes

[1] Congressional Budget Office (CBO), *The 2012 Long-term Budget Outlook*, June 2012.

[2] See CRS Report R41849, *Can Contractionary Fiscal Policy Be Expansionary?*, by Jane G. Gravelle and Thomas L. Hungerford.

[3] The 2001 and 2003 tax cuts (known as the Bush tax cuts) were temporarily extended in 2010 and are set to expire at the end of 2012; Congress may consider the fate of these tax cuts later this year. If the Bush tax cuts expire as scheduled, then tax rates will increase on ordinary income (e.g., wages and salaries), dividends, and capital gains. The House passed the Job Protection and Recession Prevention Act of 2012 (H.R. 8), which would extend all the 2001 and 2003 Bush tax cuts for another year. See CRS Report R42020, *The 2001 and 2003 Bush Tax Cuts and Deficit Reduction*, by Thomas L. Hungerford for an analysis of the Bush tax cuts.

[4] Peter Diamond and Emmanuel Saez, "The Case for a Progressive Tax: From Basic Research to Policy Recommendations," *Journal of Economic Perspectives*, vol. 25, no. 4 (Fall 2011), pp. 165-190.

[5] See CRS Report R42043, *An Analysis of the "Buffett Rule"*, by Thomas L. Hungerford for an analysis of the Buffett rule.

[6] The National Commission on Fiscal Responsibility and Reform, *The Moment of Truth*, December 2010 available at http://www.fiscalcommission.gov/sites/fiscalcommission.gov/files/documents/TheMomentofTruth12_1_2010.pdf.

[7] For more information on tax expenditures, see CRS Report RL34622, *Tax Expenditures and the Federal Budget*, by Thomas L. Hungerford; and Thomas L. Hungerford, "Tax Expenditures: Good, Bad, or Ugly?," *Tax Notes*, vol. 113,no. 4 (October 23, 2006), pp. 325-334. Recent analysis suggests that there are impediments to base broadening by modifying tax expenditures, which would not allow for significant reductions in tax rates. See CRS Report R42435, *The Challenge of Individual Income Tax Reform: An Economic Analysis of Tax Base Broadening*, by Jane G. Gravelle and Thomas L. Hungerford.

[8] In the 1970s, the top marginal tax rate on earned income was capped at 50%; only unearned income (e.g., interest and dividends) faced the 70% top marginal tax rate.

[9] See, for example, The National Commission on Fiscal Responsibility and Reform, *The Moment of Truth*, December 2010, p. 28. Support for this assertion often comes from theoretical textbook treatments, such as Robert J. Barro, *Macroeconomics*, 2nd ed. (New York: John Wiley and Sons, 1984).

[10] This is a supply side argument. See CRS Report R42111, *Tax Rates and Economic Growth*, by Jane G. Gravelle and Donald J. Marples for a discussion of these issues.

[11] Costas Meghir and David Phillips, "Labour Supply and Taxes," in *Dimensions of Tax Design: The Mirrlees Review*, ed. Stuart Adams and others (Oxford: Oxford University Press, 2010), pp. 202-274; Robert A. Moffitt and Mark O. Wilhelm, "Taxation and the Labor Supply Decisions of the Affluent," in *Does Atlas Shrug? The Economic Consequences of Taxing the Rich*, ed. Joel B. Slemrod (Cambridge, MA: Harvard University Press, 2000), pp. 193-239; Francine D. Blau and Lawrence M. Kahn, "Changes in the Labor Supply Behavior of Married Women: 1980-2000," *Journal of Labor Economics*, vol. 25, no. 3 (2007), pp. 393-438; Bradley T. Heim, "The Incredible Shrinking Elasticities: Married Female Labor Supply, 1978-2002," *Journal of Human Resources*, vol. 42, no. 4 (Fall 2007), pp. 881-918; and Kelly Bishop, Bradley Heim, and Kata Mihaly, "Single Women's Labor Supply Elasticities: Trends and Policy Implications," *Industrial and Labor Relations Review*, vol. 63, no. 1 (October 2009), pp. 146-168.

[12] Edward Gramlich, "The Importance of Raising National Saving," the Benjamin Rush Lecture, Dickinson College, PA., March 2, 2005.

[13] See Richard A. Musgrave, *The Theory of Public Finance: A Study in Public Economy* (New York: McGraw-Hill Book Company, 1959).

[14] The saving ratio is the ratio of private saving to potential GDP (the level of GDP attainable when resources are fully employed).

[15] The fitted values are the points on the straight line that best characterize the relationship between two variables.

[16] The regression results are reported in **Table A-1**. Also see CRS Report R42111, *Tax Rates and Economic Growth*, by Jane G. Gravelle and Donald J. Marples.

[17] Eric Engen, Jane Gravelle, and Kent Smetters, "Dynamic Tax Models: Why They Do the Things They Do," *National Tax Journal*, vol. 50, no. 3 (September 1997), pp. 631-656; and Organisation for Economic Co-operation and Development, *Tax and the Economy: A Comparative Assessment of OECD Countries*, Tax Policy Studies No. 6, 2001.

[18] See Edward F. Denison, *Trends in American Economic Growth, 1929-1982* (Washington: The Brookings Institution, 1985); and CRS Report RL33482, *Saving Incentives: What May Work, What May Not*, by Thomas L. Hungerford.

[19] Leonard F. Burman, *Labyrinth of Capital Gains Tax Policy: A Guide for the Perplexed* (Washington: Brookings Institution Press, 1999).

[20] For further evidence see CRS Report R42111, *Tax Rates and Economic Growth*, by Jane G. Gravelle and Donald J. Marples; and Christina D. Romer and David H. Romer, *The Incentive Effects of Marginal Tax Rates: Evidence from the Interwar Era*, National Bureau of Economic Research, Working Paper 17860, February 2012.

[21] Office of National Statistics, *The ONS Productivity Handbook*, Basingstoke, Hampshire, UK, 2007, Ch. 3, http://www.ons.gov.uk.

[22] Also see CRS Report R42111, *Tax Rates and Economic Growth*, by Jane G. Gravelle and Donald J. Marples.

[23] Immediately after World War II, the U.S. was the dominant world economy. This dominant position was gradually reduced as the European and Asian economies recovered and U.S. current account deficits grew.

[24] Statistical significance provides information on the likelihood a result occurs by chance.

[25] Eric Engen and Jonathan Skinner, "Taxation and Economic Growth," *National Tax Journal*, vol. 49, no. 4 (December 1996), pp. 617-642; and Charles W. Calomiris and Kevin A. Hassett, "Marginal Tax Rate Cuts and thePublic Tax Debate," *National Tax Journal*, vol. 55, no. 1 (March 2002), pp. 119-131.

[26] Martin Feldstein and Douglas W. Elmendorf, "Budget Deficits, Tax Incentives, and Inflation: A Surprising Lesson from the 1983-1984 Recovery," in *Tax Policy and the Economy*, ed. Lawrence H. Summers, vol. 3 (Cambridge, MA: MIT Press, 1989), pp. 1-23; William G. Gale and Samara R. Potter, "An Economic Evaluation of the Economic Growth and Tax Relief Reconciliation Act of 2001," *National Tax Journal*, vol. 55, no. 1 (March 2002), pp. 133-186; and William G. Gale and Peter R. Orszag, "Economic Effects of Making the 2001 and 2003 Tax Cuts Permanent," *International Tax and Public Finance*, vol. 12 (2005), pp. 193-232.

[27] CBO, *Trends in the Distribution of Income Between 1979 and 2007*, October 2011; CRS Report R42131, *Changes in the Distribution of Income Among Tax Filers Between 1996 and 2006: The Role of Labor Income, Capital Income, and Tax Policy*, by Thomas L. Hungerford; and CRS Report R42400, *The U.S. Income Distribution and Mobility: Trends and International Comparisons*, by Linda Levine.

[28] Thomas Piketty and Emmanuel Saez, "Income Inequality in the United States, 1913-1998," *Quarterly Journal of Economics*, vol. 118, no. 1 (February 2003), pp. 1-39, with updated tables available at http://elsa.berkeley.edu/~saez/.

[29] Michael Marmot, *The Status Syndrome: How Social Standing Affects Our Health and Longevity* (New York: Henry Holt and Co., 2004); Richard G. Wilkinson, *Unhealthy Societies: The Afflictions of Inequality* (New York: Routledge,1996); Robert Frank, *Falling Behind: How Rising Inequality Hurts the Middle-Class* (Berkeley, CA: University of California Press, 2007); and Gopal K. Singh and Mohammad Siahpush, "Widening

Socioeconomic Inequalities in US Life Expectancy, 1980-2000," *International Journal of Epidemiology*, vol. 35 (May 2006), pp. 969-979.

[30] Donald Deere and Finis Welch, "Inequality, Incentives, and Opportunity," *Social Philosophy and Policy*, vol. 19, no. 1 (2002), pp. 84-109.

[31] Milton Friedman, *Capitalism and Freedom* (Chicago: University of Chicago Press, 1962), p. 171.

[32] Note that the top 0.1% in the income distribution includes the top 0.01%. These are two different definitions of the rich. The top 0.1% represents one family in 1,000 and the top 0.01% represents one in 10,000.

[33] These trends are consistent with evidence that the income of high-income households has become more cyclical since 1980. See Jonathan A. Parker and Annette Vissing-Jorgensen, "The Increase in Income Cyclicality of High-Income Households and Its Relation to the Rise in Top Income Shares," *Brookings Papers on Economic Activity*, Fall 2010, pp. 1-55.

[34] A. B. Atkinson and Andrew Leigh, "Top Income in New Zealand 1921-2005: Understanding the Effects of Marginal Tax Rates, Migration Threat, and the Macroeconomy," *Review of Income and Wealth*, vol. 54, no. 2 (June 2008), pp. 149-165; and Thomas Piketty, Emmanuel Saez, and Stefanie Stantcheva, *Optimal Taxation of Top Labor Incomes: A Tale of Three Elasticities*, National Bureau of Economic Research, Working Paper 17616, November 2011.

[35] CRS Report R42131, *Changes in the Distribution of Income Among Tax Filers Between 1996 and 2006: The Role of Labor Income, Capital Income, and Tax Policy*, by Thomas L. Hungerford.

[36] Ibid.

[37] National income is split into the share going to labor (wages) and the share going to capital (capital income).

[38] CBO, *Trends in the Distribution of Household Income Between 1979 and 2007*, October 2011.

[39] CBO, *Trends in the Distribution of Household Income Between 1979 and 2007*, October 2011; and CRS Report R42131, *Changes in the Distribution of Income Among Tax Filers Between 1996 and 2006: The Role of Labor Income, Capital Income, and Tax Policy*, by Thomas L. Hungerford.

[40] Hacker and Pierson argue that "public officials have rewritten the rules of American politics and the American economy in ways that have benefited the few at the expense of the many." Jacob Hacker and Paul Pierson, *Winner-Take-All Politics* (New York: Simon and Schuster, 2010).

[41] Thomas Piketty, Emmanuel Saez, and Stefanie Stantcheva, *Optimal Taxation of Top Labor Incomes: A Tale of Three Elasticities*, National Bureau of Economic Research, Working Paper 17616, November 2011.

[42] Jon Bakija, Adam Cole, and Bradley T. Heim, *Jobs and Income Growth of Top Earners and the Causes of Changing Income Inequality: Evidence from U.S. Tax Return Data*, Williams College, working paper, November 2010.

[43] See Michael L. Walden, "Will Households Change Their Saving Behavior After the "Great Recession"? The Role of Human Capital," *Journal of Consumer Policy*, vol. 35 (2012), pp. 237-254.

[44] Robert J. Gordon and John M. Veitch, "Fixed Investment in the American Business Cycle, 1919-83," in *The American Business Cycle: Continuity and Change*, ed. Robert J. Gordon (Chicago: University of Chicago Press, 1986),pp. 267-357.

[45] Young Lee and Roger H. Gordon, "Tax Structure and Economic Growth," *Journal of Public Economics*, vol. 89(June 2005), pp. 1027-1083.

[46] A. B. Atkinson and Andrew Leigh, "Top Income in New Zealand 1921-2005: Understanding the Effects of Marginal Tax Rates, Migration Threat, and the Macroeconomy," *Review of Income and Wealth*, vol. 54, no. 2 (June 2008), pp. 149-165; and Thomas Piketty, Emmanuel Saez, and Stefanie Stantcheva, *Optimal Taxation of Top Labor Incomes: A Tale of Three Elasticities*, National Bureau of Economic Research, Working Paper 17616, November 2011.

In: Tax Rates
Editor: Howard P. Durham
ISBN: 978-1-62417-215-1

Chapter 2

TAX RATES AND ECONOMIC GROWTH*

Jane G. Gravelle and Donald J. Marples

SUMMARY

This report summarizes the evidence on the relationship between tax rates and economic growth, referring in a number of cases to other CRS reports providing more substance and detail. Potentially negative effects of tax rates on economic growth have been an issue in the debates about whether to extend the 2001-2003 income tax cuts, whether to increase taxes to reduce the deficit, and whether to reform taxes by broadening the base and lowering the rate.

Initially, it is important to make a distinction between the effects of policies aimed at short-term stimulation of an underemployed economy and long-run growth. In the short run, both spending increases and tax cuts are projected to increase employment and output in an underemployed economy. These effects operate through the demand side of the economy. In general, the largest effects are from direct government spending and transfers to lower-income individuals, whereas the smallest effects are from cutting taxes of high-income individuals or businesses.

Long-run growth is a supply-side phenomenon. In the long run, the availability of jobs is not an issue as an economy naturally creates jobs. Output can grow through increases in labor participation and hours, increases in

* This is an edited, reformatted and augmented version of the Congressional Research Service Publication, CRS Report for Congress R42111, dated December 5, 2011.

capital, and changes such as education and technological advances that enhance the productivity of these inputs.

Historical data on labor participation rates and average hours worked compared to tax rates indicates little relationship with either top marginal rates or average marginal rates on labor income. Relationships between tax rates and savings appear positively correlated (that is, lower savings are consistent with lower, not higher, tax rates), although this relationship may not be causal. Similarly, during historical periods, slower growth periods have generally been associated with higher, not lower, tax rates.

A review of statistical evidence suggests that both labor supply and savings and investment are relatively insensitive to tax rates. Small effects arise in part because of offsetting income and substitution effects (which make the direction of effects uncertain) and in part because each of these individual responses appears small. Institutional constraints may also have an effect. Offsetting income and substitution effects also affect savings. Capital gains taxes are often singled out as determinants of growth, but their effects on the cost of capital are quite small. International capital flows also appear to have a small effect. Most expenditures that affect the productivity of labor and capital inputs (research and development, education, or infrastructure) are already tax favored or provided by the government. Small business taxes are also sometimes emphasized as important to growth, but the evidence suggests a modest and uncertain effect on entrepreneurship.

Claims that the cost of tax reductions are significantly reduced by feedback effects do not appear to be justified by the evidence, where feedback effects are in the range of 3% to 10% and can, in some cases, be negative. Because of the estimated realizations response, capital gains tax cuts have in the past been estimated to have a large revenue offset (about 60%), but more recent empirical estimates suggest one of about 20%. In general, for stand-alone rate reductions the additions to the deficit would cause tax cuts to have a larger cost both because of debt service and because of crowding out of investment which would swamp most behavioral effects.

This report summarizes the evidence on the relationship between tax rates and economic growth, referring in a number of cases to more-detailed CRS reports. Potentially negative effects of tax rates on economic growth have been an issue in the debate about whether to extend the 2001-2003 income tax cuts, whether to increase taxes to address the budget deficit, and whether to broaden the base and lower the rates with tax reform. After first distinguishing between short-run counter-cyclical considerations and long-run growth effects, the following section provides some historical data on tax rates and measures of factor supply and growth. This report then reviews the empirical evidence on the major contributors to growth. The final section concludes with a review of dynamic scoring issues.

SHORT-RUN COUNTER-CYCLICAL EFFECTS VERSUS LONG-RUN GROWTH

Initially, it is important to make a distinction between the effects of policies aimed at short-term stimulation of an underemployed economy and long-run growth. In the short run, both spending increases and tax cuts are projected to increase employment and output in an underemployed economy, such as the United States today.[1] These effects operate through the demand side of the economy. In general, the largest effects are from direct spending and transfers to lower-income individuals, whereas the smallest effects are from cutting taxes of high-income individuals or businesses.[2]

Long-run growth is a supply-side phenomenon. In the long run, the availability of jobs is not an issue as an economy naturally creates jobs. Output can grow through increases in labor participation and hours, increases in capital, and changes such as education and technological advances that enhance the productivity of these inputs. The remainder of the report addresses this longer-term growth issue.

HISTORICAL COMPARISONS OF TAX RATES, LABOR SUPPLY, SAVINGS, AND GROWTH RATES

This section summarizes the historical insights about the effect of tax rates on economic growth and selected factors—labor force participation, savings, and growth in investment—commonly associated with economic growth. While this type of historical analysis is unable to identify causal relationships, it can offer suggestive evidence on the magnitude of the tax effect on these factors. To summarize, the evidence presented in this section suggests that past changes in tax rates have had no large clear effect on economic growth and selected factors commonly associated with economic growth.

Since much discussion is focused on the consequences of individuals in the top marginal tax rate brackets who provide much of the saving and entrepreneurial input in the economy, the following charts include examinations of the relationship between labor supply, savings, and growth rates for the top marginal rates. Similarly, there is often a particular focus on capital gains tax rates and savings so these data presented below include relationships between these variables.

Labor Force Participation

Labor force participation rates for men and women have trended in opposite directions over the past 60 years. In particular, for men the labor force participation rate has fallen by roughly 15 percentage points (from 86.4% to 71.2%), while the female labor force participation rate has risen by nearly 25 percentage points (from 33.9% to 58.6%) over the same time period. Also during the past six decades, the top marginal income tax rate on labor income has trended downward, from a high of over 90% to today's top rate of 35%. The effective marginal tax rate has fluctuated in a narrower range (between 20% and 30%), with no clear trend.[3] These relationships are shown in **Figure 1**.

Given the divergent trends in male and female labor force participation rates, it seems unlikely that the downward trend in top marginal tax rates on labor income or the more stable effective tax rate on labor income could be a driving factor concerning labor force participation rates.

Taxes could affect the hours (intensity) of work. During the 1965-2010 period (as mentioned above) the top marginal income tax rate on labor income has trended downward and the effective tax rate has fluctuated in a narrower range, while average hours worked has steadily declined (see **Figure 2**). Some multinational research provides evidence suggesting that the decrease in marginal tax rates is correlated with decreases in average hours worked.[4] This evidence should be used with caution as hours have trended smoothly downward during the period, while tax changes have been more abrupt and the composition of the U.S. work force has changed markedly.

Savings and Investment and GDP Growth

U.S. savings has been generally declining over the past 60 years. Specifically, as shown in **Figure 3**, savings as a percentage of national income has declined 14 percentage points (from a high of 12.1% in 1951 to -1.9% in 2009) during the time period.

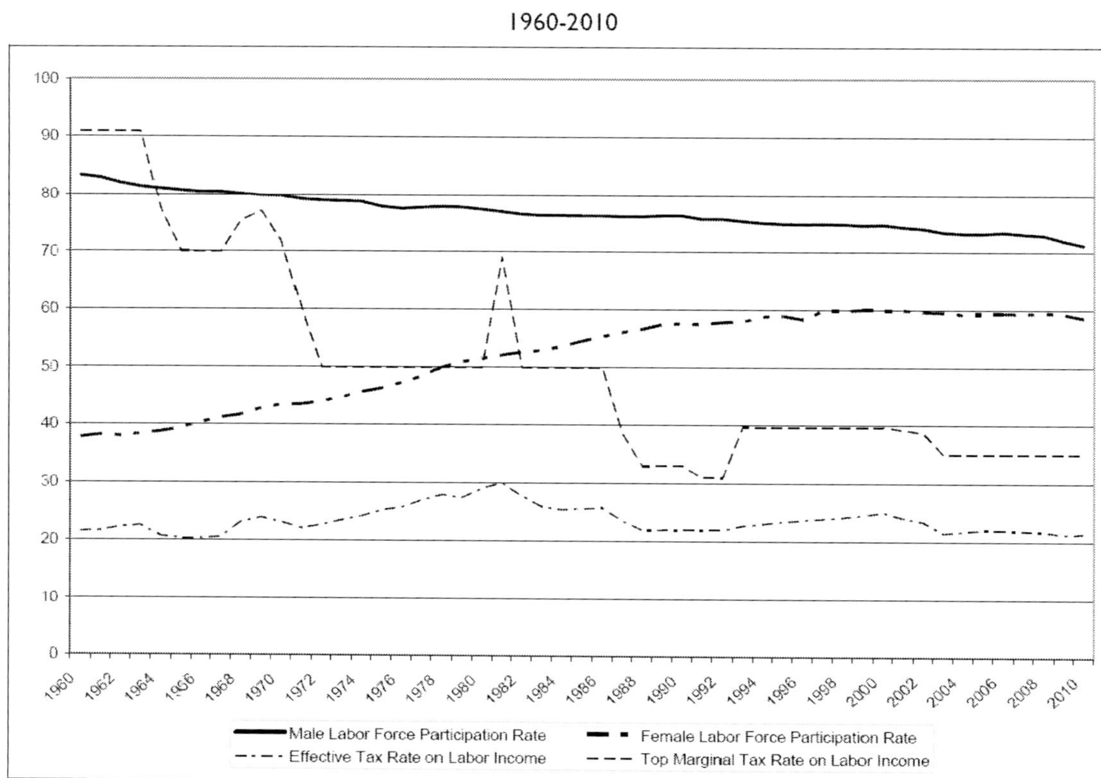

Source: Economic Report of the President, Urban-Brookings Tax Policy Center, and National Bureau of Economic Research.

Figure 1. Tax Rates and Labor Force Participation.

1965-2010

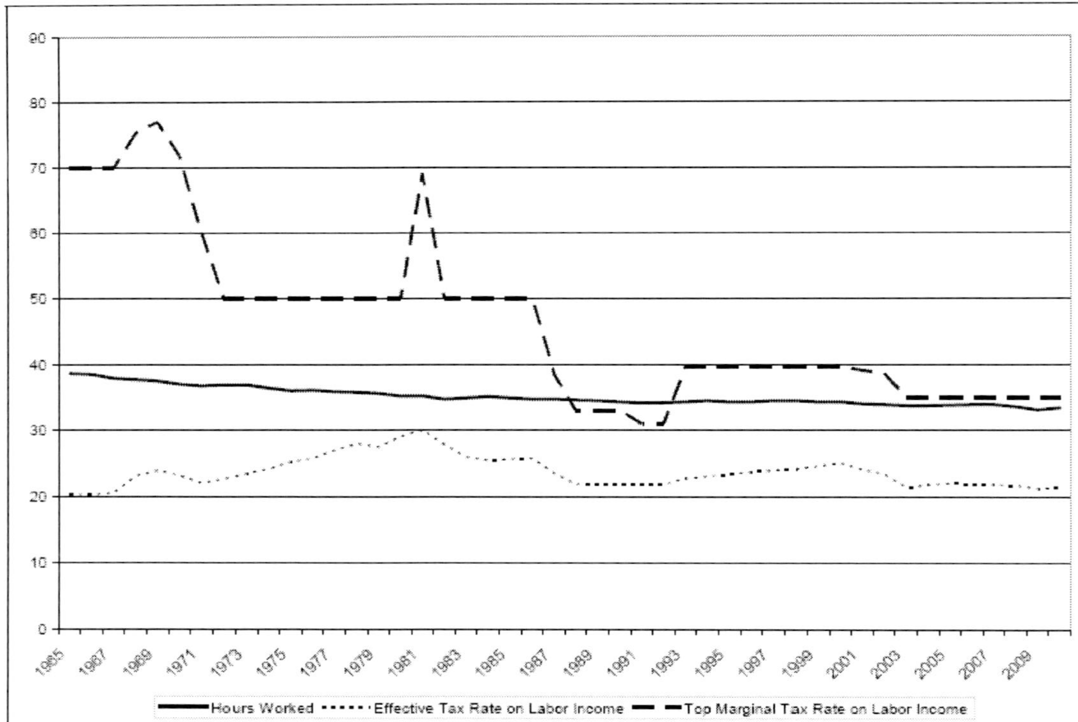

Source: Bureau of Economic Analysis, Urban-Brookings Tax Policy Center, and National Bureau of Economic Research.

Figure 2. Tax Rates and Hours Worked.

Over the same 60-year period, the top marginal income tax rate and effective tax rate of capital gains income has fluctuated. In particular, the maximum tax rate on capital gains income was 25% through most of the 1960s before rising in the 1970s, eventually reaching a high of 40% towards the end of the decade and subsequently falling to roughly 15% today. Similarly, effective tax rates on capital income fluctuated during the 1960s and 1970s before generally trending lower since the early 1980s.

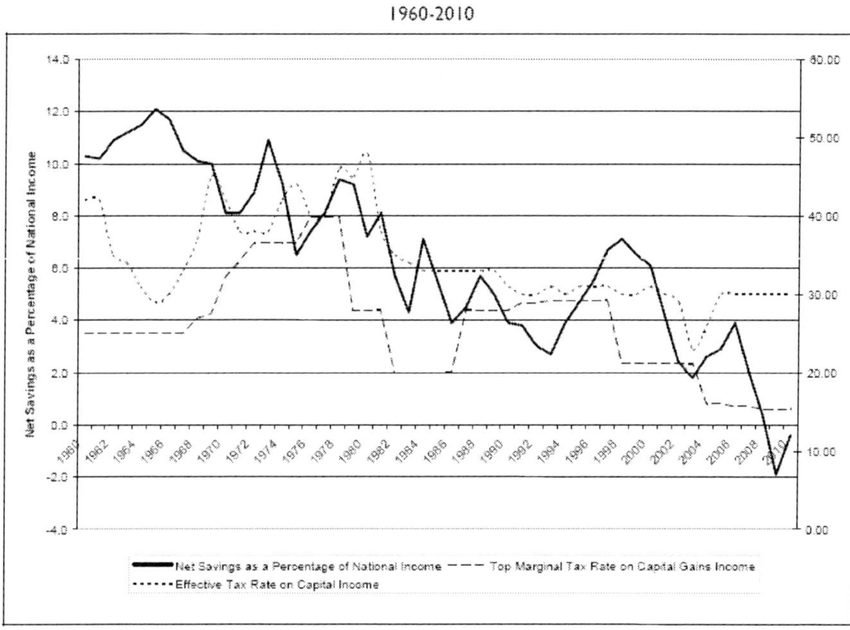

Source: CRS Report RS21706, *Historical Effective Marginal Tax Rates on Capital Income*; Bureau of Economic Analysis; and the Urban-Brookings Tax Policy Center.

Figure 3. Tax Rates and Net Savings.

Given the fluctuation in the tax rates on capital gains income along with the steady decline in broader income tax rates from **Figure 3**, it seems unlikely that changes in tax rates caused savings as a percentage of national income to steadily fall over this period. Note that maximum overall income tax rates in **Figure 1** applied to investment in unincorporated businesses and, during most of the period, to interest and dividends. During most of the 1970s, although the maximum tax rate on earned income was capped briefly at 60% and then at 50%, the tax rate on interest and dividends stayed at 70%.

Although not pictured in **Figure 3**, corporate tax rates also declined in this period, ranging between 50% and 60% in the 1950s, 40% to 50% in the 1960s and 1970s, 30% to 40% in the 1980s, and around 30% since that time.[5]

Over the past six decades, periods of higher average top tax rates appear on the surface to be related to periods of lower rates of growth in real gross domestic product (GDP) and real net fixed investment. As seen in **Table 1**, the full 60-year time period can be broken into three shorter time periods (1950-1970, 1971-1986, and 1987-2010) that correspond to periods of relatively high, moderate, and low taxes on labor income (and moderate, high, and low taxes on capital gains). The data show that real GDP growth and real growth in net fixed investment have each declined over the time period, suggesting that periods of lower taxes are not associated with higher rates of economic growth or increases in investment.

One concern when using a long historical view for economy-wide analysis is that the choice of time periods may lead to misleading conclusions, as the size and composition of the economy today differs in many ways from the economy in the 1950s. To examine whether this lack of an apparent clear relationship between top tax rates and the rate of economic growth is due to changes in the economy over time, a shorter time period can be used.

Table 1. Average Top Tax Rates on the Growth Rate of Real GDP and Real Net Fixed Investment, by Time Period 1950-2010

	Average Top Marginal Income Tax Rate on Labor Income	Average Top Marginal Tax Rate on Capital Gains Income	Rate of Growth in Real GDP	Rate of Growth in Real Net Fixed Investment
1950-1970	84.8%	25.6%	3.86%	0.93%
1971-1986	51.8%	30.2%	2.94%	0.32%
1987-2010	36.4%	23.0%	2.85%	0.23%

Source: BEA and the Urban-Brookings Tax Policy Center.

Table 2 decomposes the most recent time period from **Table 1** into three shorter time periods (1987-1992, 1993-2002, and 2003-2007) that correspond to periods of relatively low, high, and moderate income tax rates. Note that the average top marginal income tax rates in **Table 2** are more tightly clustered than the tax rates in **Table 1** and the time period used ends before the recent recession. Again the data do not appear to support a clear relationship between lower taxes and higher economic growth; if anything, they suggest the opposite (although we do not believe that relationship is causal, in light of other evidence presented in the following section).

Table 2. Average Top Income Tax Rate on the Growth Rate of Real GDP 1987-2007

	Average Top Marginal Income Tax Rate	Rate of Growth in Real GDP
1987-1992	33.3%	2.31%
1993-2002	39.5%	3.68%
2003-2007	35.0%	2.79%

Source: BEA and the Urban-Brookings Tax Policy Center.

Review of Evidence on Factors Affecting Growth

This section summarizes the theoretical insights and empirical evidence on the forces driving output and growth which supplement the information provided in the historical comparisons. More detailed discussion of various issues is contained in cited CRS reports.

Labor Supply[6]

An increase in wages or a decrease in taxes may increase or decrease labor supply. The increased after-tax income will, in theory, promote the consumption of more leisure which reduces labor supply, while the substitution effect (labor effort now pays more) promotes an increase in labor supply. The outcome depends on the strength of these opposing forces and is an empirical matter.

Empirical evidence has generally found small and uncertain labor supply effects from higher wages. Historical evidence over a long period of time suggests that increased wages result in less work. In 1856 the average workweek was 70 hours, which had declined to 40 hours a week by 1940. Participation has declined for men, although it has increased for women (which may be related to changes in social norms, birth control, marriage, and economies in household production). Econometric studies have found small, and often negative, labor supply responses for men. In the past, a larger and positive response has been found for women, especially married women, but more recent research has indicated small responses for women as well; women are increasingly becoming more like men in their response.[7]

Marginal tax rate reductions are more likely than average tax rate reductions to induce a positive supply response because marginal reductions have greater proportional effects on substitution than on income, although this difference becomes small at very high income levels. In general, however, tax cuts still lead to similar effects as wages because both income and substitution effects are small. A study specifically focusing on the affluent found that tax changes have no measurable effect on the labor supply of high income men, who tend to be relatively unresponsive.[8]

Savings and Investment Response[9]

The effect of taxes on savings is also, in theory, ambiguous. While substitution effects cause a preference for future consumption that increases savings, income effects mean that a given target can be achieved with smaller savings because the after-tax return is larger.

Empirical evidence suggests a negligible and possibly negative savings response. Historically the savings rate had been relatively constant until the early 1980s, after which it declined. It declined at the point that reductions in capital income taxes and an expansion of tax preferred savings vehicles (such as individual retirement accounts) were enacted. Studies that examined the savings rate over time found results that were small in magnitude, but uncertain in direction, with a central tendency suggesting no response. Moreover, even at the highest of these elasticity estimates, the savings response would have a very modest effect on output. Completely eliminating capital income taxes would increase output by 4/10 of 1% after 10 years and 9/10 of 1% after 25 years. In the latter case the average increase is 4/100 of 1% per year, or about 1% to 2% of normal growth rate.[10]

Inter-temporal models, which are popular with academic researchers, sometimes predict large savings responses to certain tax changes, but these models are complex and highly stylized, making assumptions that individuals have perfect information and foresight, and are affected by various assumptions built into the model.[11]

In a closed economy, capital accumulation depends on domestic saving. In an open economy capital can be increased by investment from abroad although the benefits of that inflow are largely captured by foreigners. This inflow would generally not be affected by individual income taxes but could be affected by corporate rate cuts. These estimates are also small, given the imperfect mobility of capital and size of the capital stock. The effect of a ten-percentage point cut in the corporate income tax is estimated to eventually increase output by about 15/100 of 1% of output, but U.S. citizens would have a benefit of less than 2/100 of 1% of output.[12]

Sometimes the capital gains tax is singled out as being particularly important to savings.[13] However, this tax is no different from any other tax on capital income, and its share of the tax burden is relatively small. According to estimates of tax rates, moving from a 15% to a 20% tax on capital gains would raise the tax rate on corporate equity capital from 34.7% to 35.2%, about 6/10 of a percentage point. The change would raise the overall tax rate in the economy (since corporate equity is about a third of capital) by about 2/10 of 1%. It would change the overall cost of capital before tax by about 6 basis points. These effects take into account that about half of equity income is in tax-preferred savings accounts.[14]

Technological Progress, Innovation, and Small Business

The same factors of production (labor and capital) can lead to larger output with technological and productivity enhancements. These factors include technological advances, organizational innovations (one historical example is the assembly line), education and training of the labor force, and public infrastructure. Economists are less able to determine the causes of technological advances and organizational innovation (accidental discovery, results of spending on research, etc.). Investment in research and development are, however, favorably treated by the tax code: most research costs are deducted when incurred, which is the same as a zero tax rate on the return to capital, and they are also eligible for a credit. Education is also favorably treated and education and infrastructure are supported by public spending and loan guarantees.[15]

Some arguments have been made that raising the top rates may especially harm small businesses who create most of the jobs. However, as noted earlier, job creation is a short-term issue. In any case, an examination of the evidence suggests that small businesses do not create a disproportionate share of jobs, that only a small fraction of unincorporated businesses would be affected by changes in the two top rates (around 2% to 3%), and that 80% of the reduced taxes are likely to accrue to non-business income and almost 90% to either non-business income or businesses without employees. Finally, while evidence is mixed, most evidence suggests that higher tax rates encourage self-employment.[16]

In summation, the evidence in this section suggests that changing tax rates is likely to have small effects on supply of labor and capital and on output.

Dynamic Revenue Estimating

Claims that the cost of tax reductions is significantly reduced through feedback effects, because of increases in economic growth (and that gains from tax increases are significantly reduced) have been made. As indicated in the previous analysis, however, these effects are limited.[17] While various dynamic models can potentially produce larger results, the models with responses most consistent with empirical evidence suggest a revenue feedback effect of about 1% for the 2001-2004 Bush tax cuts.[18] Feedback effects could arise from shifts of taxable income outside of changes in real output (such as increasing itemized deductions such as charitable contributions, realizing more income in fringe benefits, and similar responses). A series of studies providing direct relationships between tax rates and tax revenues designed to measure these responses initially found large effects. Subsequent critiques of the methodological problems with these studies and new estimates found much smaller results. Another problem with this approach is that it would vary depending on the type of tax change (for example, feedback effects would be less likely for a tax increase that broadened the base than from a rate increase). In any case, the evidence suggests feedback effects from 3% to 10%.[19] In addition, studies that estimated significant responses to two important types of tax provisions, charitable contributions and capital gains, have recently been found to be much smaller.[20]

Capital gains taxes have been scored for some time as having a significant feedback effect through changes in realizations, one that had a revenue offset of around 60%. More recent estimates, however, have suggested a feedback effect of about 20%.[21]

Claims have been made that a corporate rate cut would pay for itself through capital flows from abroad. However, using estimates from an international general equilibrium model with capital flow responses consistent with empirical evidence to simulate a ten percentage point cut in the corporate tax rate, this factor offset corporate revenue losses by about 5%.[22]

Any positive feedback effects would be much more than offset, for a stand-alone tax change, by the interest and crowding out effects of debt. For example, in the corporate rate cut, interest payments increased the effect of the change on the deficit by 25% in the budget horizon, and reduced output from crowding out reduced revenue by another 20%.

End Notes

[1] See CRS Report R41332, *Economic Recovery: Sustaining U.S. Economic Growth in a Post-Crisis Economy*, by Craig K. Elwell for further information on the current state of the U.S. economy.

[2] See multipliers in Table 1 and Table 2 of CRS Report R41849, *Can Contractionary Fiscal Policy Be Expansionary?*, by Jane G. Gravelle and Thomas L. Hungerford.

[3] The effective tax rate is the rate applied to the last dollar of labor income and is thus a marginal rate.

[4] Lee Ohanian, Andrea Raffo, and Richard Rogerson, *Long Term Changes in Labor Supply and Taxes: Evidence from OECD Countries, 1956-2004*, The Federal Reserve Bank of Kansas City-Economic Research Department, December 2006.

[5] CRS Report RS21706, *Historical Effective Marginal Tax Rates on Capital Income*, by Jane G. Gravelle.

[6] Labor supply is reviewed in CRS Report RL31949, *Issues in Dynamic Revenue Estimating*, by Jane G. Gravelle.

[7] See Bradley T. Heim, "The Incredible Shrinking Elasticities: Married Female Labor Supply, 1978-2002, *Journal of Human Resources*, Vol. 42, No. 4, Fall 2007, pp. 881-918; Kelly Bishop, Bradley Heim, and Kata Mihaly, "Single Women's Labor Supply Elasticities: Trends and Policy Implications." *Industrial and Labor Relations Review*. Vol. 63 No. 1, October, 2009, pp.146-168.

[8] See Robert A. Moffitt and Mark O. Wilhelm, "Taxation and the Labor Supply Decisions of the Affluent," In *Does Atlas Shrug? the Economic Consequences of Taxing the Rich*," Ed. Joel B. Slemrod, Russell Sage Foundation, New York, pp. 193-239.

[9] Savings response is also reviewed in CRS Report RL31949, *Issues in Dynamic Revenue Estimating*, by Jane G. Gravelle. See also CRS Report RL33378, *Would Tax Reform Alter the Economy's Growth?*, by Marc Labonte and CRS Report RL33482, *Saving Incentives: What May Work, What May Not*, by Thomas L. Hungerford.

[10] These estimates are in Eric Engen, Jane Gravelle, and Kent A. Smetters, "Dynamic Tax Models: Why They Do the Things They Do," National Tax Journal, Vol. 50, No. 3, September 1997, pp. 631-656.

[11] In addition to assuming perfect foresight and perfect information, and a variety of arbitrary assumptions (such as hours available for work), these models do not allow for marriage and, where labor is variable, barriers to entering and leaving the work force. These models in some cases cannot permit recessions, since the perfect equilibrium and information means there is no involuntary unemployment. Note also that in the short term, effects on savings from reducing taxes on capital income arise from shifting labor supply through time in response to rates of return, a response that seems unlikely given the consequences for employment of a spotty work history. For further technical discussion, in addition to CRS Report RL31949, *Issues in Dynamic Revenue Estimating*, by Jane G. Gravelle, see Eric Engen, Jane Gravelle, and Kent A. Smetters, "Dynamic Tax Models: Why They Do the Things They Do," *National Tax Journal*, Vol. 50, No. 3, September 1997, pp. 631-656.

[12] CRS Report R41743, *International Corporate Tax Rate Comparisons and Policy Implications*, by Jane G. Gravelle.

[13] For additional discussion see CRS Report R40411, *The Economic Effects of Capital Gains Taxation*, by Thomas L. Hungerford.

[14] These estimates assume that the effective corporate tax rate is 30%, that half of capital gains are never realized and assets where gains are realized are held for five years, that the real return to equity after corporate tax is 7%, that dividends are 4% and the inflation rate is 2%. The effects would be twice as large if marginal investment is assumed to be financed only from taxable accounts. For further discussion of measuring effective tax rates see CRS Report RS21706, *Historical Effective Marginal Tax Rates on Capital Income*, by Jane G. Gravelle.

[15] One major cost of education is foregone earnings, which are not affected by taxes. There are also a number of education and training tax benefits such as the tuition tax credit.

[16] CRS Report R41392, *Small Business and the Expiration of the 2001 Tax Rate Reductions: Economic Issues*, by Jane G. Gravelle.

[17] See CRS Report RL31949, *Issues in Dynamic Revenue Estimating*, by Jane G. Gravelle for a general discussion.

[18] See CRS Report RL33672, *Revenue Feedback from the 2001-2004 Tax Cuts*, by Jane G. Gravelle, p. 7-11.

[19] See CRS Report RL33672, *Revenue Feedback from the 2001-2004 Tax Cuts*, by Jane G. Gravelle.

[20] See CRS Report R41364, *Capital Gains Tax Options: Behavioral Responses and Revenues*, by Jane G. Gravelle and CRS Report R40518, *Charitable Contributions: The Itemized Deduction Cap and Other FY2011 Budget Options*, by Jane G. Gravelle and Donald J. Marples.

[21] CRS Report R41364, *Capital Gains Tax Options: Behavioral Responses and Revenues*, by Jane G. Gravelle.

[22] CRS Report R41743, *International Corporate Tax Rate Comparisons and Policy Implications*, by Jane G. Gravelle.

In: Tax Rates
Editor: Howard P. Durham

ISBN: 978-1-62417-215-1

Chapter 3

AN ANALYSIS OF THE "BUFFETT RULE"*

Thomas L. Hungerford

SUMMARY

Warren Buffett, the chairman of Berkshire Hathaway, noted that he paid 17.4% of his taxable income in income and payroll taxes—"a lower percentage than was paid by any of the other 20 people" in his office. He stated that "the mega-rich pay income taxes at a rate of 15 percent on most of their earnings but pay practically nothing in payroll taxes." Within a month, the Obama Administration unveiled a plan for economic growth and deficit reduction. The Administration stated that one of its principles for tax reform was to observe the "Buffett rule"—"no household making over $1 million annually should pay a smaller share of its income in taxes than middle-class families pay." In October 2011, Senator Harry Reid introduced the American Jobs Act of 2011 (S. 1660), which contains a 5.6% surtax on millionaires to pay for the provisions of the jobs bill. On March 22, Senator Whitehouse introduced a bill to reduce the deficit by imposing a minimum tax on high-income taxpayers (S. 2230). This report examines the Buffett rule, but uses a measure of income that captures the ability to pay taxes and incorporates the effect of the corporate income tax in addition to the individual income tax and the payroll tax.

---

* This is an edited, reformatted and augmented version of the Congressional Research Service Publication, CRS Report for Congress R42043, dated March 28, 2012.

The results of this analysis show that the current U.S. tax system violates the Buffett rule in that a large proportion of millionaires pay a smaller percentage of their income in taxes than a significant proportion of moderate-income taxpayers. Roughly a quarter of all millionaires (about 94,500 taxpayers) face a tax rate that is lower than the tax rate faced by 10.4 million moderate-income taxpayers (10% of the moderate-income taxpayers). Tax reforms that are consistent with the Buffett rule would likely include raising tax rates on capital gains and dividends. For example, the President has proposed allowing the 2001 and 2003 Bush tax cuts to expire for high-income taxpayers and taxing carried interests of hedge fund managers as ordinary income as tax reforms that observe the Buffett rule. Research suggests that these tax reforms are unlikely to affect many small businesses or to deter saving and investment.

In August 2011, Warren Buffett, the chairman of Berkshire Hathaway, published an opinion piece in the *New York Times*.[1] He noted that he paid 17.4% of his taxable income in income and payroll taxes—"a lower percentage than was paid by any of the other 20 people" in his office. He stated that "the mega-rich pay income taxes at a rate of 15 percent on most of their earnings but pay practically nothing in payroll taxes." He proposed that tax rates be raised for taxpayers making more than $1 million.

One month later, the Obama Administration unveiled a plan for economic growth and deficit reduction.[2] The Administration stated that one of its principles for tax reform was to observe the "Buffett rule"—"no household making over $1 million annually should pay a smaller share of its income in taxes than middle-class families pay."[3] The reaction to the Buffett rule tax reform principle was swift, with some accusing the President of engaging in class-warfare.[4] In October 2011, Senator Harry Reid introduced the American Jobs Act of 2011 (S. 1660), which contains a 5.6% surtax on millionaires to pay for the provisions of the jobs bill. On March 22, Senator Whitehouse introduced a bill to reduce the deficit by imposing a minimum tax on high-income taxpayers (S. 2230). This report examines the validity of the Buffett rule and the issues surrounding the rule.

INDIVIDUAL INCOME TAXES AND PAYROLL TAXES

To calculate tax liability on the 1040 tax form, a taxpayers first adds up income from taxable sources; some income is excluded from taxes such as public assistance benefits, interest income from state and local bonds, 401(k) contributions and earnings, and some or all of Social Security benefits. Next the taxpayer subtracts various deductions available to all taxpayers (called above-the-line deductions), exemptions for the taxpayer and dependents, and either the standard deduction or itemized deductions.

The taxpayer then calculates regular income tax liability based on tax tables or worksheets.[5] The individual income tax in the U.S. uses a progressive tax formula with tax rates increasing from 10% to 35% as taxable income increases. Taxpayers with long-term capital gains and qualified dividends face a tax rate of either 0% or 15% depending on the taxpayer's tax bracket (lower income taxpayers in the 10% and 15% tax brackets face a 0% rate on long-term capital gains and qualified dividends).[6] Higher-income taxpayers also have to calculate the alternative minimum tax (AMT).[7] These taxpayers pay the higher of the regular income tax or AMT. Lastly, tax credits are subtracted to get the total tax due to the government.

Workers also pay payroll taxes on wages and salaries. These taxes fund the Social Security and Medicare programs. The total Social Security payroll tax rate is 12.4% and applies to all wages below $106,800.[8] The Medicare payroll tax rate is 2.9% on all wages. Other income is not subject to payroll taxes.[9]

THE SIMPLE BUFFETT RULE

Figure 1 displays the range of tax rates (individual income and payroll tax rates combined) for various income categories based on taxable income. The tax rates are the effective average tax rate with respect to taxable income (total tax divided by taxable income)—the tax rates Warren Buffett referred to in his op-ed piece. Overall, the combined tax is regressive in that the average tax rate decreases as taxable income increases. Taxpayers with taxable income below $100,000 pay on average about 35% of their taxable income in taxes while taxpayers with taxable income above $1 million pay on average less than 30%.

The average tax rate for all taxpayers in an income category hides a great deal of variation in the tax rates the taxpayers actually face. The vertical lines show the range in tax rates from the 10th percentile to the 90th percentile. The tax rate at the 10th percentile is the tax rate such that 10% of the taxpayers pay a lower tax rate and 90% of the taxpayers pay a higher tax rate. For taxpayers with taxable income less than $100,000 (moderate-income taxpayers), 10% face a tax rate of less than 14.2%, and another 10% of these moderate-income taxpayers face tax rates exceeding 48.9%.[10] Interestingly, 65% of rich taxpayers (i.e., taxable income over $1 million)—about 200,000 taxpayers—face a tax rate lower than the median tax rate of moderate-income taxpayers. The primary reason for this is the higher-income taxpayers with low tax rates receive a very high proportion of the income from long-term capital gains and qualified dividends, which are taxed at low tax rates and not subject to payroll taxes. Lower-income taxpayers with relatively high tax rates receive most of their income from wages, which are subject to payroll taxes.

The Buffett Rule with a Broader Measure of Income and Taxes

Taxable income is a fairly narrow measure of income and does not reflect all the resources available to the taxpayer or gage the taxpayer's ability to pay taxes. This is because personal exemptions and itemized deductions have been subtracted. This can artificially increase the effective average tax rate faced by a taxpayer. Adjusted gross income (AGI) is a broader income measure that does not exclude personal exemptions and itemized deductions for charitable contributions, state taxes, and mortgage interest.[11] AGI is used for the analysis in calculating tax rates and determining income categories.

The preceding analysis also excluded the corporate income tax, which is often used as justification for reduced tax rates on certain types of income. Specifically, one of the arguments for the reduced tax rates on long-term capital gains and qualified dividends is to reduce double taxation since this income may also be subject to the corporate income tax. Taxes from all sources should be included in an analysis of the effective tax burden and this analysis considers the individual income tax, the corporate income tax, and the payroll tax.[12] But three issues need to be addressed regarding the burden of the corporate income tax.[13]

The first issue is the question of who actually bears the burden of the corporate income tax. Several recent studies estimate that most or all of the burden of the corporate income falls on labor through reduced wages. These studies, however, have been shown to suffer from various methodological deficiencies.[14] The evidence suggests that most or all of the burden of the corporate income tax falls on owners of capital.[15] In the analysis, it is assumed that 100% of the corporate income tax falls on capital income (dividends and capital gains), which mostly affects high-income taxpayers (almost 60% of all capital gains and dividends are received by taxpayers with income over $1 million).

Second, not all of this income is taxed at the corporate level. The Internal Revenue Service (IRS) reports that a substantial proportion of capital gains and losses (short-term and long-term) reported by taxpayers are passthrough gains or losses (that is, the income is not reported on any corporate tax form and passes directly to individual taxpayers to report on their individual income tax form), gains or losses from the sale of government bonds, and other assets never taxed at the corporate level.[16] For example, hedge funds are generally organized as partnerships. Under current tax law, a partnership does not pay income taxes; instead gains and losses flow through to the partners who include it on their income tax returns.

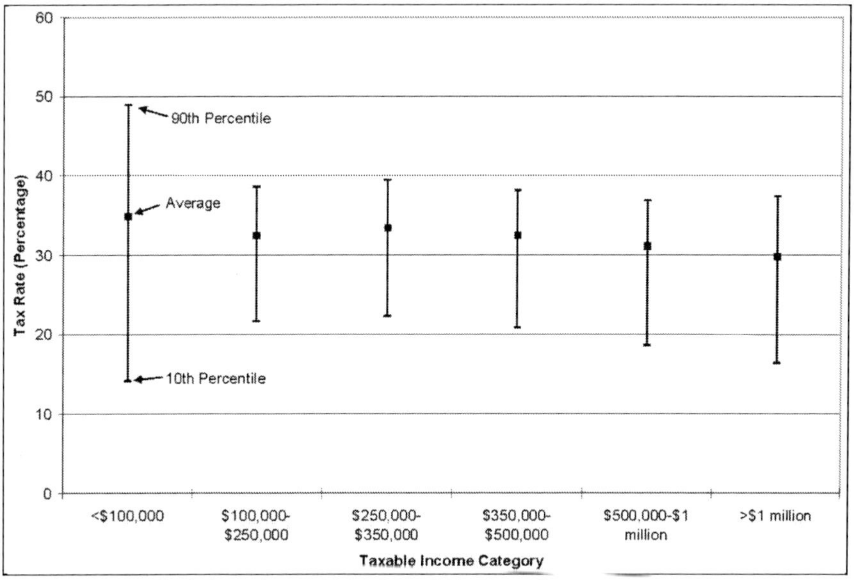

Source: CRS analysis based on 2006 SOI Public Use File.
Notes: Numerical tax rates are reported in **Table A-2**.

Figure 1. Tax Rates by Taxable Income Category.

The income from the partnership is often taxed as capital gains or qualified dividends at reduced tax rates (i.e., 15%). Essentially, if the partnership earns long-term capital gains or qualified dividends, the income flows through to the partners as long-term capital gains or qualified dividends and is taxed accordingly—the income is not recharacterized (e.g., from capital gains to ordinary income) as it passes through from the partnership to the individual partners. Some partners receive partnership interests in exchange for contributions of capital (that is, investments) and are referred to as limited partners; some partners receive partnership interests in exchange for services (carried interests) and these are general partners who actively manage the partnership.[17] Most of this income is taxed at the reduced long-term capital gains rate and is not taxed at the corporate level.[18] It is estimated that 37.4% of net capital gains are taxed at the corporate level as well as the individual level (such as corporate stock, mutual funds, and capital gains distributions). It is also assumed that all dividends are taxed at both the corporate and individual levels.

The third issue concerns the corporate tax rate. The statutory corporate tax rate in 2010 was 39.2%, which includes federal and state corporate taxes. However, several studies estimate the effective corporate tax rate is between 22.2% and 27.1%.[19] After subtracting out the state corporate tax rate from the highest estimate, it is assumed that the effective corporate tax rate is 24.2%.

Figure 2 displays the effective tax rates for various AGI categories. The "hi-inc" level varies depending on the taxpayer's filing status: $200,000 for single taxpayers; $250,000 for married taxpayers filing a joint return; and $125,000 for married taxpayers filing separate returns. Individual income taxes, corporate taxes, and payroll taxes are included and the income base for the tax rate calculation is AGI. Average taxes are progressive except at the top: the average tax rate increases with income except for taxpayers with income over $5 million. As before, the mean tax rate obscures a great deal of variation in tax rates faced by taxpayers in each income category. Although the mean tax rate for moderate-income taxpayers with AGI below $100,000 is 18.95%, 10% face a tax rate greater than 26.5% (about 10.4 million taxpayers) and another 10% pay less than 9% of their income in taxes.

Among millionaires (see the last two categories in the figure), the average tax rate is almost 30% with about 10% facing a tax rate greater than 35%. Furthermore, another 10% face a tax rate below 24%. Comparing millionaires with moderate-income taxpayers (with AGI less than $100,000), roughly one-quarter of all millionaires (about 94,500 taxpayers) face a tax rate that is lower than the tax rate faced by 10.4 million moderate-income taxpayers (10% of the moderate-income taxpayers), which would be considered a violation of the Buffett rule but not to the extent alluded to by Mr. Buffett.

ISSUES

The President has proposed allowing the 2001 and 2003 Bush tax cuts expire for high-income taxpayers and taxing carried interests as ordinary income as one way to observe the Buffett rule.[20] Critics of using the Buffett rule as a principle of tax policy argue that raising tax rates on millionaires, especially capital gains tax rates, will harm job creators—small business—and deter saving and investment. These arguments are evaluated in turn.

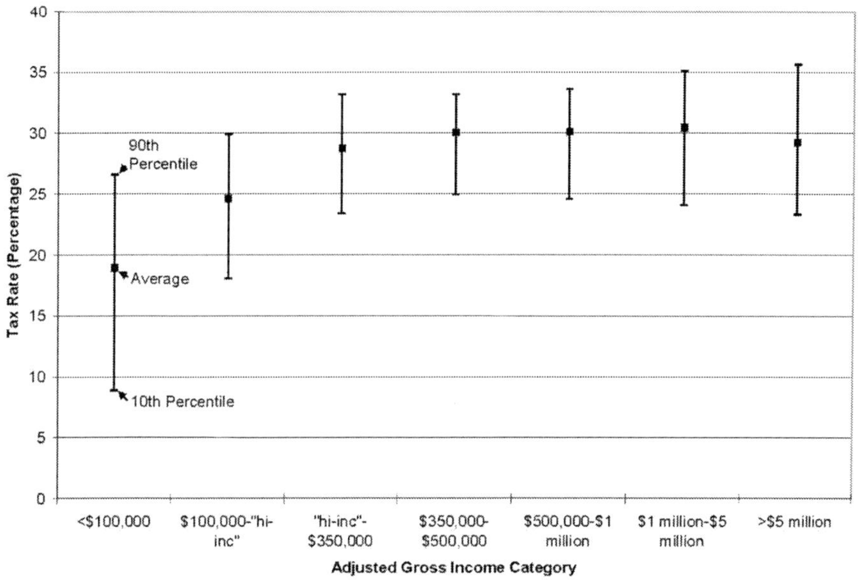

Source: CRS analysis based on the 2006 SOI Public Use File.

Notes: "hi-inc"=$200,000 for single taxpayers; $250,000 for married taxpayers filing joint return; and $125,000 for married taxpayers filing a separate return. Numerical tax rates are reported in **Table A-3**.

Figure 2. Tax Rates by Adjusted Gross Income Category.

Small Business and Job Creation

Small business owners are difficult to identify from publicly available income tax records.[21] As a substitute, analysts often identify taxpayers reporting business income or losses on their tax return (on the Schedule C, E, or F form). This method likely overstates the number of small business owners since some of this business income is simply a return on passive investments. Using this method, about 30.9 million taxpayers can be identified as small business owners. About 72% of the taxpayers reporting business income also report receiving wage income.[22] **Table 1** reports the proportion of taxpayers with business income and the distribution of tax rates among these taxpayers. Most taxpayers with business income (74%) have AGI below $100,000. About 1% of the returns with business income have AGI over $1 million. For these rich taxpayers, the average tax rate is 29.1%, but about one-quarter face a tax rate of less than 26.5% (the 90th percentile tax rate for all taxpayers with AGI less than $100,000)—again, an apparent violation of the Buffett rule. The small share of taxpayers with small business income in the millionaire category suggests that tax reform policies designed to ensure adherence to the Buffett rule will affect few small businesses.

Table 1. Tax Rates of Business Owners by Adjusted Gross Income Category Taxpayers Reporting Business Income

AGI Category	Percent Distribution of Business Owners	Tax Rates			
		Mean	10th Percentile	Median	90th Percentile
Less than $100,000	74.0	18.70	8.02	17.57	27.35
$100,00-"hi-inc"	18.9	23.91	16.29	24.81	29.84
"hi-inc"-$350,000	2.9	28.48	22.89	29.07	32.98
$350,000-$500,00	1.6	29.95	24.73	30.22	33.26
$500,000-$1 million	1.6	29.91	24.45	29.94	33.56
$1 million-$5 million	0.9	30.27	24.06	30.82	34.88
Greater than $5 million	0.1	29.05	23.25	29.46	35.37

Source: CRS analysis based on the 2006 SOI Public Use File (see Appendix for a description of the data).

Notes: "hi-inc"=$200,000 for single taxpayers; $250,000 for married taxpayers filing joint return; and $125,000 for married taxpayers filing a separate return.

Many observers claim that small businesses are the primary creators of jobs.[23] Most research cited by these observers is from the 1980s. More recent research suggests that small businesses contribute only slightly more jobs than larger business relative to their employment share.[24] The difference, however, appears to be due to hiring by new startup firms rather than to existing small businesses.[25] New startup firms also account for a great deal of job destruction and within five years about 40% of the new jobs created by startups have disappeared because of business failure.[26] Firms generally do not generate much business income in their first years in operation; consequently, most small business owners of startup firms are not in the top income categories and would not be affected by tax policies that observe the Buffett rule.[27]

Saving and Investment

Tax reforms that satisfy the Buffett rule likely would include an increase in the tax rate on long-term capital gains and qualified dividends. Some argue that raising these tax rates will reduce saving and investment. National saving is made up of saving by the government (public saving) and by households and firms (private saving). Public saving is equal to the government's deficit or surplus—it is negative for a deficit and positive for a surplus. Increasing capital gains tax rates would likely increase public saving because it increases tax revenues without affecting outlays; this decreases a budget deficit or increases a budget surplus.[28]

Households save by investing in their own business or investing in stocks, bonds, and other financial instruments. Changing capital gains tax rates changes the after-tax rate of return on investments (for example, increasing the tax rate decreases the after-tax return). The change in the rate of return has two offsetting effects on saving. Decreasing the rate of return can decrease households' willingness to save (the substitution effect). But at the same time, the decreased return may induce households to save more to maintain their desired or target wealth level (the income effect). Consequently, the effect of capital gains taxes on private saving is likely to be small.

The traditional economic theory of saving, the life-cycle model, assumes that individuals make rational, far-sighted decisions. The preponderance of empirical evidence, however, does not support the life-cycle model.[29] Behavioral theories of saving emphasize the role of inertia, the lack of self-control, and the limit of human intellectual capabilities. To cope with the complexities involved in making saving decisions, individuals often use simple rules of thumb and develop target levels of wealth. Once their target level of wealth is obtained, many individuals suspend active saving.[30] Saving rates have fallen over the past 30 years while the capital gains tax rate has fallen from 28% in 1987 to 15% today (0% for taxpayers in the 10% and 15% tax brackets). This suggests that changing capital gains tax rates have had little effect on private saving.

Some have argued that preferential capital gains tax rates would boost high risk investments such as in venture capital. Most venture capital, however, is supplied by pension funds, college endowments, foundations, and insurance companies—sources not associated with the capital gains tax. In 2003, only about 10% of investors in venture capital funds were individuals and families.[31]

Capital gains tax rate increases appear to increase public saving and may have little or no effect on private saving. Consequently, capital gains tax increases likely have a positive overall impact on national saving and investment.

CONCLUDING REMARKS

The Obama Administration has stated it will adopt the Buffett rule as one of its principles for tax reform. This rule basically follows from the well-known tax principles of vertical equity and ability to pay, which suggest that a tax system should at least be proportional (all taxpayers pay the same percentage of income in taxes) if not progressive (the tax rate increases with income). The results of this analysis show that the current U.S. tax system violates the Buffett rule in that a large proportion of millionaires pay a smaller percentage of their income in taxes than a significant proportion of moderate-income taxpayers. Tax reforms that are consistent with the Buffett rule would likely include raising tax rates on capital gains and dividends. For example, the President has proposed allowing the 2001 and 2003 Bush tax cuts expire for high-income taxpayers and taxing carried interests as ordinary income as one way to observe the Buffett rule. Research suggests that these reforms are unlikely to affect many small businesses or to deter saving and investment.

APPENDIX. DATA

The source of data is the 2006 Internal Revenue Service (IRS) Statistics of Income (SOI) Public Use File. The Public Use File is a nationally representative sample of tax returns for the 2006 tax year. To protect the identity of individual taxpayers while preserving the character of the data, the IRS made changes to the data. Consequently, while reliable aggregate information can be obtained, individual taxpayer records in the data may or may not contain information from just one tax return. The unit of analysis is the tax return for a taxpayer, and IRS-provided sample weights are used throughout the analysis. The analysis sample contains information for 130,438 taxpayers (representing 122.7 million taxpayers).

Income was adjusted to 2010 values using the GDP personal consumption expenditure deflator. Tax liability was calculated using a tax module prepared by the author based on the 2010 form 1040 as well as other forms and schedules of the regular income tax and alternative minimum tax (AMT). Taxpayers with negative or zero adjusted gross income are omitted from the analysis. The refundable portion of tax credits were not considered in the analysis. This does not, however, affect the results of the analysis.

Table A-1. Number of Sample Observations

AGI Category	Unweighted Number	Weighted	
		Number	Percent
Less than $100,000	55,247	104,441,369	85.13
$100,000-"hi-inc"	19,753	14,911,280	12.15
"hi-inc"-$350,000	7,350	1,587,809	1.29
$350,000-$500,000	6,532	718,425	0.59
$500,000-$1 million	12,199	644,724	0.53
$1 million-$5 million	24,929	336,237	0.27
Greater than $5 million	4,428	44,207	0.04
All	130,438	122,684,051	100.00

Source: CRS analysis based on the 2006 SOI Public Use File.

Notes: "hi-inc"=$200,000 for single taxpayers; $250,000 for married taxpayers filing joint return; and $125,000 for married taxpayers filing a separate return.

Table A-2. Tax Rates by Taxable Income Category

Income Category	Mean	10th Percentile	Median	90th Percentile
Less than $100,000	34.89	14.15	35.11	48.93
$100,000-$250,000	32.51	21.64	34.12	38.59
$250,000-$350,000	33.42	22.31	35.58	39.48
$350,000-$500,000	32.46	20.82	34.88	38.12
$500,000-$1 million	31.15	18.59	34.28	36.88
Greater than $1 million	29.76	16.37	33.60	37.40

Source: CRS analysis based on the 2006 SOI Public Use File.

Table A-3. Tax Rates by Adjusted Gross Income Category

AGI Category	Mean	10th Percentile	Median	90th Percentile
Less than $100,000	18.95	8.89	17.84	26.58
$100,00-"hi-inc"	24.63	18.08	25.29	29.91
"hi-inc"-$350,000	28.76	23.39	29.41	33.20
$350,000-$500,00	30.06	24.94	30.48	33.18
$500,000-$1 million	30.12	24.59	30.22	33.63
$1 million-$5 million	30.47	24.09	31.11	35.10
Greater than $5 million	29.25	23.30	29.85	35.63

Source: CRS analysis based on the 2006 SOI Public Use File.

Notes: "hi-inc"=$200,000 for single taxpayers; $250,000 for married taxpayers filing joint return; and $125,000 for married taxpayers filing a separate return.

End Notes

[1] Warren E. Buffett, "Stop Coddling the Super-Rich," *New York Times*, August 14, 2011, p. A.

[2] Office of Management and Budget, *Living Within Our Means and Investing in the Future*, Washington, DC, September 2011.

[3] Ibid., p. 46.

[4] For example, Representative Paul Ryan, chairman of the House Budget Committee, reportedly said on Fox News in reference to the Buffett rule, "class warfare ... may make for really good politics, but it makes for rotten economics" (http://www.foxnews.com/politics/2011/09/18/rep-ryan-accuses-obama-waging-class-warfare-with-millionaire-tax-plan/).

[5] For more information, see CRS Report RL33755, *Federal Income Tax Treatment of the Family*, by Jane G. Gravelle.

[6] Long-term capital gains are gains on the sale of assets held for a year or more. See CRS Report R40411, *The Economic Effects of Capital Gains Taxation*, by Thomas L. Hungerford.

[7] For more information on the AMT, see CRS Report RL30149, *The Alternative Minimum Tax for Individuals*, by Steven Maguire.

[8] Both the employee and employer pay half of the tax on wages. It is generally agreed by economists that the employer's share of the tax is borne by the employee. See CBO, *Effective Federal Tax Rates, 1979-1997*, October 2001.

[9] The Patient Protection and Affordable Care Act (P.L. 111-148) included an additional payroll tax of 0.9% on high-income workers and a 3.8% Medicare tax on investment income of high-income taxpayers beginning in 2013. For more information, see CRS Report R41128, *Health-Related Revenue Provisions in the Patient Protection and Affordable Care Act (ACA)*, by Janemarie Mulvey.

[10] Buffett notes that the other people in his office faced tax burdens of 33% to 41% with an average of 36%.

[11] AGI does exclude the above-the-line deductions as well as certain income such as public assistance and 401(k) contributions.

[12] See CBO, *Average Federal Tax Rates in 2007*, June 2010.

[13] In addressing these issues, various assumptions need to be made regarding the burden of the corporate income tax. In cases where different decisions regarding assumptions could be made, the one that would "bias" against finding a Buffett rule result was chosen.

[14] See CRS Report RL34229, *Corporate Tax Reform: Issues for Congress*, by Jane G. Gravelle and Thomas L. Hungerford; and Jennifer C. Gravelle, *Corporate Tax Incidence: A Review of Empirical Estimates and Analysis*, CBO working paper 2011-01, June 2011, for reviews of these studies and an analysis of their deficiencies.

[15] Ibid.

[16] Janette Wilson and Pearson Liddell, "Sales of Capital Assets Reported on Individual Tax Returns, 2007," *Statistics of Income Bulletin*, Winter 2010, pp. 75-104.

[17] See CRS Report RS22689, *Taxation of Hedge Fund and Private Equity Managers*, by Mark Jickling and Donald J. Marples; and CRS Report RS22717, *Taxation of Private Equity and Hedge Fund Partnerships: Characterization of Carried Interest*, by Donald J. Marples.

[18] About 45% of net capital gains are from passthrough net gains or a transaction involving partnership, S corporation, and estate or trust interests.

[19] CRS Report R41743, *International Corporate Tax Rate Comparisons and Policy Implications*, by Jane G. Gravelle.

[20] Office of Management and Budget, *Living Within Our Means and Investing in the Future*, Washington, DC, September 2011, pp. 47-48. The Obama Administration has proposed to designate a general partner's share of partnership income that is not attributable to invested capital as ordinary income, which would be taxed at the higher individual income tax rates rather than at the reduced capital gains tax rate. In addition, this share of income would be subject to self-employment taxes. For more information on the Bush tax cuts see CRS Report R42020, *The 2001 and 2003 Bush Tax Cuts and Deficit Reduction*, by Thomas L. Hungerford.

[21] See Matthew Knittel, Susan Nelson, and Jason DeBacker, et al., *Methodolgy to Identify Small Businesses and Their Owners*, Office of Tax Analysis, U.S. Department of Treasury, OTA Technical Paper 4, Washington, DC, August 2011 for more information on the difficulty of identifying small business owners.

[22] Some of the wage income could be from the working spouse of a business owner. Also, the business income could be from selling Amway or Mary Kay products on the side.

[23] CRS Report R41392, *Small Business and the Expiration of the 2001 Tax Rate Reductions: Economic Issues*, by Jane G. Gravelle.

[24] Ibid.

[25] Ibid.

[26] John C. Haltiwanger, Ron S. Jarmin, and Javier Miranda, *Who Creates Jobs? Small vs. Large vs. Young*, National Bureau of Economic Research, Working Paper no. 16300, Cambridge, MA, August 2010.

[27] About 90% of small businesses that have been in operation for less than nine years have sales revenue of less than $1 million. Business income is revenue less costs. If revenue is less than $1 million then business income will be less than $1 million. See Traci L. Mach and John D. Wolken, "Financial Services Used by Small Business: Evidence from the 2003 Survey of Small Business Finances," *Federal Reserve Bulletin*, October 2006, p. A188.

[28] See Jane G. Gravelle, "Can A Capital Gains Tax Cut Pay for Itself," *Tax Notes*, vol. 48 (July 9, 1990), pp. 209-219.

[29] For a discussion and citations to the literature see CRS Report RL33482, *Saving Incentives: What May Work, What May Not*, by Thomas L. Hungerford.

[30] F. Thomas Juster, Joseph P. Lupton, James P. Smith, and Frank Stafford, "The Decline in Household Saving and the Wealth Effect," *Review of Economics and Statistics*, vol. 87, no. 4 (November 2005), pp. 20-27.

[31] National Venture Capital Association, *Venture Impact*, 4th Edition, 2007, available at http://www.nvca.org/pdf/NVCA_VentureCapital07-2nd.pdf.

In: Tax Rates
Editor: Howard P. Durham

ISBN: 978-1-62417-215-1

Chapter 4

THE 2001 AND 2003 BUSH TAX CUTS AND DEFICIT REDUCTION*

Thomas L. Hungerford

SUMMARY

A series of tax cuts were enacted early in the George W. Bush Administration by the Economic Growth and Tax Relief Reconciliation Act of 2001 (EGTRRA) and the Jobs and Growth Tax Relief Reconciliation Act of 2003 (JGTRRA). These tax cuts, which are collectively known as the Bush tax cuts, were originally scheduled to expire at the end of 2010. These tax provisions were extended until the end of 2012 at an estimated cost of $408 billion. Beginning in 2013, many of the individual income tax parameters (such as tax rates) will revert back to 2000 levels. One legislative proposal introduced in the 112th Congress, H.R. 6104 (introduced by Representative Cedric Richmond), would extend the 2001, 2003, and 2009 tax cuts for taxpayers with income below $500,000 for another year. A proposal by Senator Harry Reid (S. 3393) would extend the tax cuts for taxpayers with income below $200,000 (for singles) or $250,000 (for married couples) for another year, but set a top income tax rate on qualified dividends of 20%.

The 2010 debate over the fate of the Bush tax cuts took place when the economy was underperforming, the unemployment rate was high, and the

* This is an edited, reformatted and augmented version of the Congressional Research Service Publication, CRS Report for Congress R42020, dated July 18, 2012.

federal deficit was large. The U.S. economy was in a severe recession from December 2007 to June 2009. The unemployment rate reached a high of 10.2% in October 2009, and it is currently still over 8%. As a result of reduced economic activity and government efforts to stimulate the economy, the federal budget deficit increased from 1.2% of GDP in FY2007 to 9.9% of GDP in FY2009. Most economic forecasts suggest the economic and budget outlook will likely be characterized by high unemployment, sluggish economic growth, and relatively large budget deficits. Consequently, the 2012 debate over the fate of the Bush tax cuts is also likely to take place in a bleak economic and fiscal environment.

There are several options that Congress may consider regarding the Bush tax cuts, and each of the options strikes a different balance between fostering economic growth and restoring fiscal sustainability. Allowing the Bush tax cuts to expire as scheduled will somewhat improve the fiscal condition by increasing tax revenue, but could retard the economic recovery. At the other extreme, permanently extending all of the Bush tax cuts would not undercut the economic recovery, but would somewhat worsen the longer-term fiscal outlook and possibly signal a lack of progress in dealing with the long-term fiscal situation. Permanently extending the Bush tax cuts could increase federal debt by almost $3 trillion over the next 10 years.

It is often argued that increasing tax rates will reduce consumer spending in the short term, and work effort, saving and investment—all key components of economic growth—in the long term. In an underemployed economy, short-term spending increases and tax cuts are expected to facilitate job creation, reduce unemployment, and increase output. The main argument against allowing the Bush tax cuts to expire at the end of 2010 was the weak recovery and the fear of pushing the economy back into recession, an argument likely to be made in 2012. Once the economy has recovered from the recession, however, long-term economic growth will be facilitated by increasing work effort, saving, and investment. It is often argued that increasing tax rates will reduce these long-term economic growth components. Economic research, however, suggests that modest tax rate increases would have little negative impact on long-term economic growth and job creation.

A series of tax cuts were enacted early in the George W. Bush Administration by the Economic Growth and Tax Relief Reconciliation Act of 2001 (EGTRRA; P.L. 107-16) and the Jobs and Growth Tax Relief Reconciliation Act of 2003 (JGTRRA; P.L. 108-27). These tax cuts, which are collectively known as the Bush tax cuts, were originally scheduled to expire at the end of 2010. In addition to the Bush tax cuts, two tax provisions enacted in the American Recovery and Reinvestment Act of 2009 (ARRA; P.L. 111-5)—an increase in the earned income tax credit and an increase in eligibility for the refundable portion of the child tax credit—were scheduled to expire at the end of 2010. In a lame-duck session in December 2010, the Bush tax cuts and the two ARRA provisions were extended for two years at an estimated cost of $408 billion.[1] Beginning in 2013, many of the individual income tax parameters (such as tax rates) are scheduled to revert back to 2000 levels. One legislative proposal introduced in the 112th Congress, H.R. 6104 (introduced by Representative Cedric Richmond), would extend the 2001, 2003 and 2009 tax cuts for taxpayers with income below $500,000 for another year. A proposal by Senator Harry Reid (S. 3393) would extend the tax cuts for taxpayers with income below $200,000 (for singles) or $250,000 (for married couples) for another year, but set a top income tax rate on qualified dividends of 20%.

The pending expiration of the Bush tax cuts generated a great deal of attention in 2010 as reflected by editorials and opinion pieces in national newspapers, and congressional hearings. The proposals regarding the Bush tax cuts were generally not about whether to let the tax cuts expire as scheduled, but rather about which tax cuts to extend and for how long. Many policy makers argued that raising taxes could impede the fragile economic recovery from the severe 2007-2009 recession.

The major tax provisions in EGTRRA and JGTRRA and the tax provisions in ARRA that are part of the current debate over the Bush tax cuts are the reduced individual income tax rates, the reduction of the marriage penalty (and increase in the marriage bonus), the repeal of the personal exemption phaseout and the limitation on itemized deductions, the reduced tax rates on long-term capital gains and qualified dividends, and expanded tax credits. Other provisions that were included in EGTRRA and JGTRRA, such as the estate tax, are not considered in this study. This report examines the Bush tax cuts within the context of the current and long-term economic and budgetary environment.

THE ECONOMIC ENVIRONMENT

The recession beginning in December 2007 is the most severe recession since the Great Depression and has been referred to as the Great Recession. Between the fourth quarter of 2007 and the second quarter of 2009, the economy shrank with real gross domestic product (GDP) falling by 5.1%. The unemployment rate increased from 4.9% in December 2007 to 10.1% by October 2009, and still is over 8%. As a result of reduced economic activity and government efforts to stimulate the economy, the federal budget deficit increased from 1.2% of GDP in FY2007 to 9.9% of GDP in FY2009. The economic recovery, however, remains fragile and the labor market has not recovered.

Two common measures of weakness in the labor market are the unemployment rate and the proportion of the labor force that has been unemployed for at least six months (the long-term unemployed). **Figure 1** displays the monthly unemployment and long-term unemployment rates since 1948. The long-term unemployment rate has generally tracked the unemployment rate over the business cycle. Over a business cycle, the long-term unemployment rate is at its lowest point at or near the beginning of a recession and then reaches a peak a few months after the end of the recession (typically within six months). Like the unemployment rate, the long-term unemployment rate is a lagging indicator—the labor market does not begin to recover from the recession until some time after the official end of the recession. After the 1990-1991 and 2001 recessions, however, the long-term unemployment rate did not reach its peak until 15 months and 19 months, respectively, after the recession ended. The long-term unemployment rate is currently higher than at any time over the past 62 years—in June 2012, 3.5% of the labor force or about 42% of the unemployed had been out of work for six months or more.

The economic outlook over the next few months is not bright and will likely be characterized by high unemployment and sluggish economic growth. For example, the Blue Chip consensus forecast has the unemployment rate staying above 8% until through 2012.[2] And Carmen Reinhart and Vincent Reinhart show that real per capita GDP growth rates tend to be low during the decade following a severe financial crisis and synchronous world-wide shocks.[3]

THE BUDGETARY ENVIRONMENT

Before the Bush tax cuts were enacted, the Congressional Budget Office (CBO) projected gradually rising federal budget surpluses—from 2.7% of GDP in 2001 to 5.3% of GDP by 2011.[4] Within a few years, CBO was projecting budget deficits. The Bush tax cuts, with a $1 trillion 10-year price tag, contributed to this shift from budget surpluses to deficits. Other major contributing factors included the 2001 recession, the increase in defense spending for the wars in Iraq and Afghanistan, and the Medicare prescription drug benefit (enacted in the Medicare Prescription Drug, Improvement, and Moderation Act of 2003; P.L. 108-173). By the time the 2007-2009 recession started, CBO was projecting deficits between FY2008 and FY2011 equivalent to over 1% of GDP (with budget surpluses after 2011).[5]

Nonetheless, federal budget conditions before the 2007-2009 recession were not much different from the conditions before previous recessions. **Figure 2** shows the budget deficit as a percentage of GDP for three years—the fiscal year before the start of the recession, the fiscal year in which the recession started, and the next fiscal year. The 2007-2009 recession is compared with the average of the prior six recessions. In the year before the Great Recession (2006), the budget deficit was 1.2% of GDP compared with 1.6% of GDP, on average, for the previous six recessions.

The situation, however, is very different for the next two fiscal years. The federal deficit increased to 3.2% of GDP in the year the 2007-2009 recession started (compared with 1.4% of GDP for previous recessions) and then to almost 10% of GDP in the next year (compared with 2.2% of GDP in previous recessions). The dramatic increase in the federal deficit after 2007 is due to the depth of the recession and the federal government's efforts to promote economic recovery, such as the Economic Stimulus Act of 2008 (P.L. 110-185) and the American Recovery and Reinvestment Act of 2009 (P.L. 111-5).

The deficit is just one facet of the fiscal condition. Another is federal debt held by the public. **Figure 3** displays federal debt held by the public as a percentage of GDP from 1790 to 2011 and CBO's baseline projection for 2011 to 2021. Federal debt in 2009 was equal to 53% of GDP—a level higher than at any time in U.S. history except for World War II. Between 2007 and 2009, federal debt increased by almost 17% of GDP. Most large increases in debt have been due to wars (the Civil War, World War I, and World War II) and to the Great Depression, but debt also increased dramatically between 1981 and 1994—by 23%—when taxes were reduced and defense spending increased. Debt as a percentage of GDP is expected to fall after 2013 in CBO's baseline projection as the economy strengthens and after the Bush tax cuts expire and the alternative minimum tax (AMT) reverts back to its 2000 parameters and affects a larger proportion of taxpayers.[6]

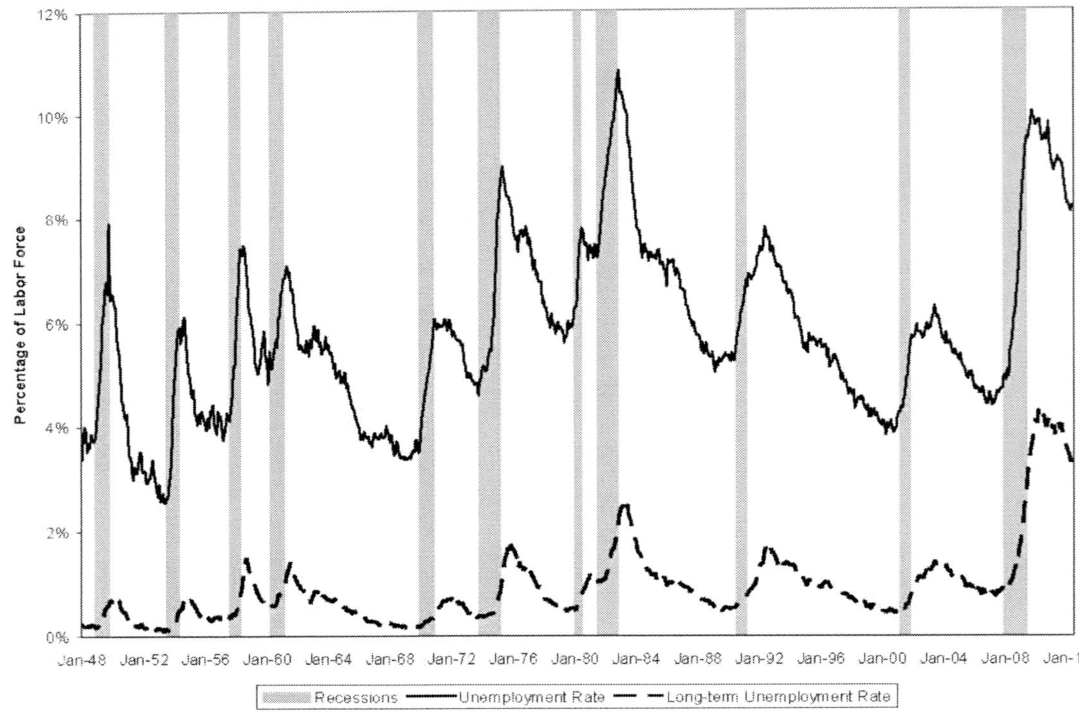

Source: CRS analysis of Bureau of Labor Statistics data.

Figure 1. Monthly Unemployment Rate and Long-Term Unemployment Rate, 1948-2012.

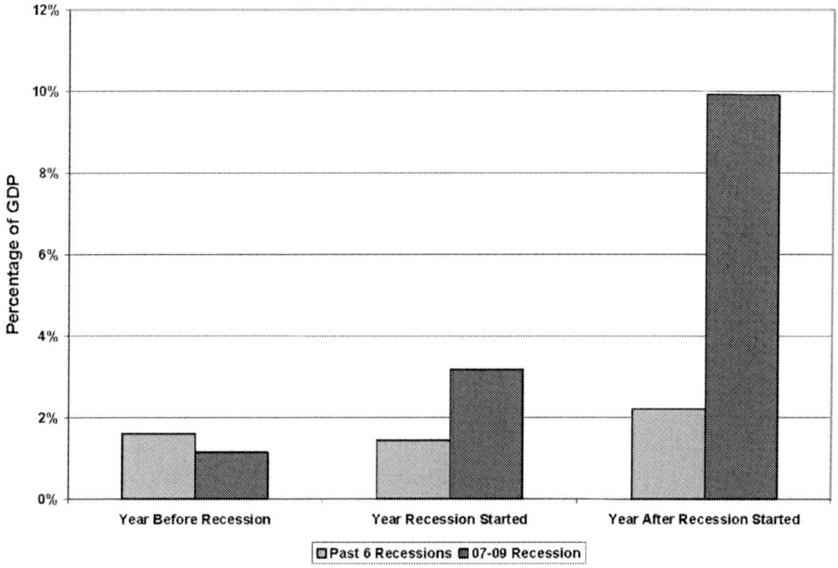

Source: CRS calculations based on OMB data.

Figure 2. Deficits as a Percentage of GDP, 2007-2009 Recession Compared with Prior Recessions.

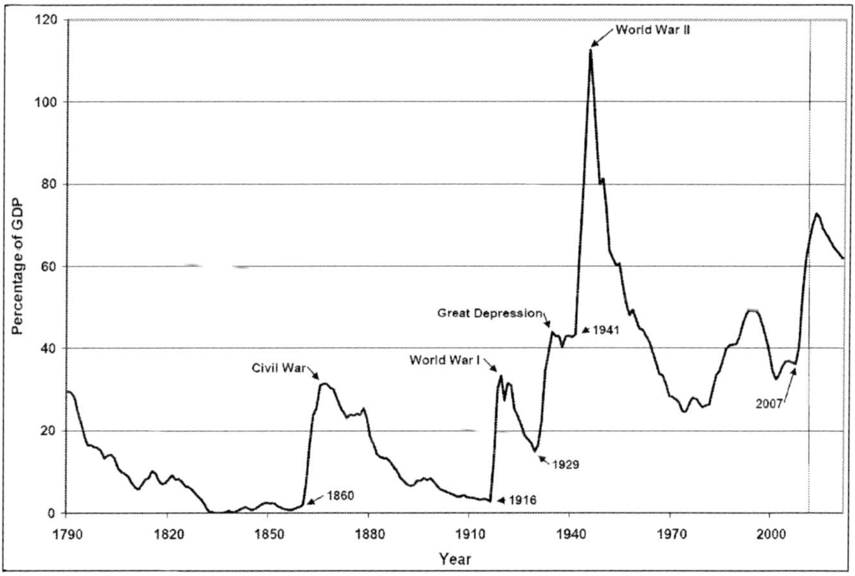

Source: CBO and OMB.

Figure 3. Debt Held by the Public as a Percentage of GDP, 1790-2021.

The United States has been running budget deficits since 2002, but has been running particularly large budget deficits since 2008. This has occurred because of the severe 2007–2009 recession and the turmoil in the financial and housing markets, which increased spending and reduced revenues due to the automatic stabilizers triggered by the recession, and legislation passed in response to the recession. After the economic recovery picks up steam, the relatively large budget deficits are unlikely to be replaced with budget surpluses. The main reasons are the steady increase in real per capita health care spending, which affects Medicare and Medicaid, and the retirement of the large baby-boom generation, which affects the two health care programs as well as Social Security. Of course, it is very difficult to predict the future course of the economy and defense needs.

In a long-term budget projection, CBO projects budget deficits and federal debt for the next 75 years under two fiscal scenarios.[7] The first scenario is the baseline or current law. This scenario assumes that current law is not changed, discretionary spending grows with inflation until 2021 and then with GDP thereafter, and Medicare spending will be constrained somewhat by the "sustainable growth rate" (SGR) mechanism, which would control the fees paid for physician's services.

The second scenario is CBO's alternative fiscal scenario. This scenario is basically a current policy scenario where discretionary spending grows with GDP, the Bush tax cuts are extended and the AMT is indexed until 2021 with revenues remaining as a constant share of GDP thereafter, and Medicare's payment rate for physicians remains at current levels. Many argue this is a more realistic picture of the future budget than the baseline scenario.

Under the baseline scenario, publicly held debt increases from its current level to 84% of GDP by 2035 and then remains fairly constant thereafter. Under CBO's alternative fiscal scenario, however, debt as a percentage of GDP reaches 109% of GDP by 2023 (about the same level as in 1946) and 190 % of GDP by 2035—extraordinary levels that are unprecedented for the United States. If the effects of slower growth due to higher debt levels under the alternative fiscal scenario are incorporated, the debt-to-GDP ratio could reach 250%.[8]

The Bush Tax Cuts

Several tax provisions were included in EGTRRA, JGTRRA, and ARRA. However, only a few are the focus of debate:

- the 10%, 25%, and 28% tax rates—the 10% tax rate was introduced and the 28% and 31% tax rates were reduced to 25% and 28%, respectively;
- the 33% and 35% tax rates—the 36% and 39.6% tax rates were reduced to 33% and 35%, respectively;
- the reduced marriage penalty—expanded the 15% tax bracket and increased the standard deduction for couples;
- the repeal of the personal exemption phaseout (PEP) and the limitation on itemized deduction (Pease)—both PEP and Pease were gradually phased out and eliminated in 2010;[9]
- the reduced long-term capital gains tax rate—tax rate was reduced from 10% and 20% to 0% and 15%;[10]
- the reduced tax rate on qualified dividends—qualified dividends are taxed at long-term capital gains tax rates rather than at the same tax rates as ordinary income; and
- the expanded tax credits—the child tax credit, the earned income tax credit (EITC), and education incentives were expanded.[11]

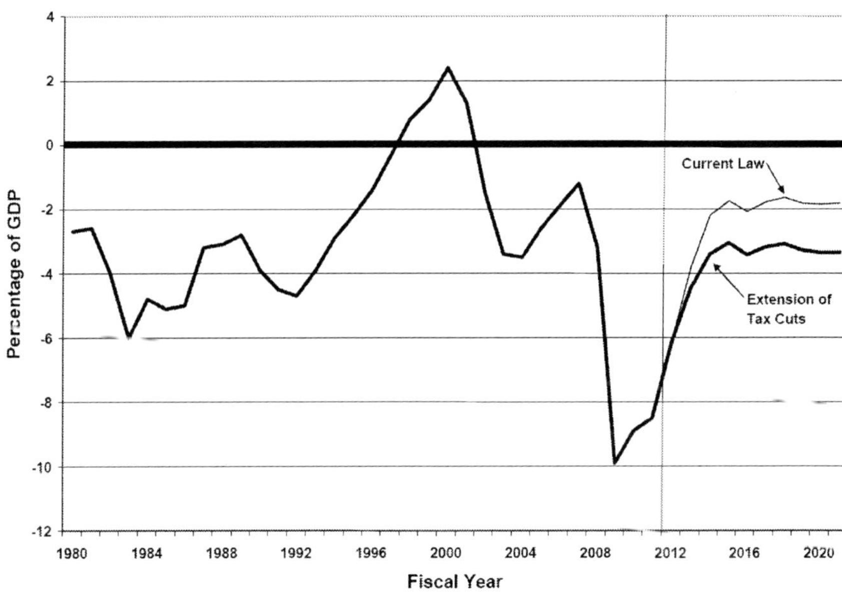

Source: CRS analysis of CBO and JCT estimates.

Figure 4. Federal Surpluses(+)/Deficits(-) as a Percentage of GDP, Two Scenarios.

The Bush tax cuts are currently scheduled to expire at the end of 2012, and the tax parameters revert back to their 2000 values (the current law baseline). **Figure 4** displays the trend in federal deficits as a percentage of GDP from 1980 to 2021. Under current law, the federal deficit is projected to decline from 8.5% of GDP in 2011 to less than 2% of GDP in 2021. If the Bush tax cuts are permanently extended, the deficit is projected to be 3.4% of GDP in 2021. This projection, however, does not take into consideration likely annual changes to the alternative minimum tax (AMT), with a projected 10-year cost of about $1,500 billion. Under CBO's baseline projection, the 10-year (FY2012-FY2021) total federal budget deficit is $3,487 billion. The projected 10-year deficit total jumps to $8,134 billion if the Bush tax cuts are extended at least through 2021 and the AMT is indexed for inflation.

Revenue Cost from Extending the Bush Tax Cut Provisions

The estimated budgetary costs of permanently extending the provisions of the Bush tax cuts are reported in **Table 1**. Over five years (FY2013-FY2017), extending the provisions are estimated to reduce tax revenues by $1,022 billion. The 10-year (FY2013-FY2022) revenue loss is estimated to be $2,375 billion. Debt service costs associated with permanently extending the Bush tax cuts are also reported in **Table 1**. Over the 10-year budget window, debt service costs are estimated to be $451 billion. Furthermore, the AMT, which is likely to be indexed to inflation, interacts with the extension of the Bush tax cuts. The last row of **Table 1** reports the combined costs of indexing the AMT, extending the Bush tax cuts, and associated debt service, which is estimated to be $4,761 billion over 10 years—more than double the total projected budget deficits over that period.

Distributional Effects of the Bush Tax Cut Provisions

The various provisions making up the Bush tax cuts have different distributional impacts. **Table 2** reports what the percentage change in after-tax income for each the tax provision would be in 2012.[12] The baseline is a situation in which the Bush tax cuts had been allowed to expire. This estimate provides information on who benefits from each provision and by how much. The Suits index is also calculated and reported for each provision. The Suits index is a measure of the progressivity of tax benefits and varies between -1 (completely regressive) and +1 (completely progressive).[13] The Suits index is negative (and tax benefits are regressively distributed) if the benefits from the provision are predominately received by taxpayers in the upper part of the income distribution. It is positive if the benefits predominately go to lower-income taxpayers. It is zero if the benefits are proportionately distributed throughout the income distribution.

The second and third columns in **Table 2** report the distributional effects of extending the reduced tax rate provisions. The two columns split the tax rate reductions into those targeting lower- and middle-income taxpayers and those targeting high-income taxpayers. Extending the 10%, 25%, and 28% tax rates benefits taxpayers throughout the income distribution (see column 2). The Suits index is slightly positive (0.0895) but is much closer to zero than to one—the benefits are slightly progressive but close to being proportional. The benefits of extending the 33% and 35% tax rates are entirely confined to the richest 5% of taxpayers (see column 3) and the richest 1% would see their after-tax income increase by about 2% (or about $21,500). The Suits index is −0.7979, suggesting that the benefits are highly regressive.

Extending the repeal of PEP and Pease would also benefit high-income taxpayers (the richest 5%)—the benefits are very regressively distributed (the Suits index is −0.7325). The reduced tax rates on capital gains and dividends (see columns 5 and 6) primarily benefit upper-income taxpayers and are regressively distributed. The reduced rates on capital gains benefits the upper 60% of the income distribution but the richest 1% see the largest increase in after-tax income while the reduced dividends tax rates benefits the upper 20%. In both cases, the Suits index is negative.

Extending the reduction in the marriage penalty would benefit married taxpayers throughout the income distribution. The Suits index is 0.1048 suggesting that the benefits are slightly progressive, but close to being proportional. The extension of the expanded tax credits primarily benefits taxpayers below the 80th percentile in the income distribution. The Suits index (0.6733) shows that the benefits are progressively distributed.

With the benefits of the different tax provisions accruing to taxpayers in different parts of the income distribution, decisions regarding the Bush tax cut provisions will affect income inequality. In a recent article, Hungerford examined the impacts of various tax provisions (including selected provisions of the Bush tax cuts) on income inequality.[14] The results show that the reduction in the tax rates increased income inequality as did the reduction in the capital gains and dividends tax rate, and the repeal of PEP and Pease. Both the child tax credit and earned income tax credit (EITC) reduce income inequality.

Table 1. Revenue Estimates of Bush Tax Cut Provisions: Effect on Deficit FY2013-FY2022 (billions of dollars)

Provision	2013	2014	2015	2016	2017	2018	2019	2020	2021	2022	2013-17	2013-22
American Opportunity Tax Credit	-2.5	-12.4	-12.5	-12.6	-13.1	-13.4	-14.0	-14.3	-14.8	-15.2	-53.1	-124.8
Education Provisions	-0.8	-1.8	-1.9	-2.0	-2.1	-2.2	-2.2	-2.4	-2.5	-2.6	-8.6	-20.5
Child Tax Credit	-7.0	-45.6	-46.2	-46.9	-47.2	-47.7	-48.0	-48.2	-48.4	-49.9	-192.9	-435.1
Earned Income Tax Credit	-0.1	-10.0	-10.2	-10.3	-10.5	-10.7	-10.8	-11.0	-11.1	-11.4	-41.1	-96.1
Reduced Marriage Penalty	-4.7	-6.7	-6.4	-6.2	-6.0	-5.7	-5.4	-5.2	-5.0	-5.2	-30.0	-56.5
10% Tax Rate	-31.9	-45.8	-46.0	-46.2	-46.1	-45.9	-45.8	-45.6	-45.4	-46.8	-216.0	-445.5
25, 28, 33, and 35% Tax Rates	-37.1	-56.9	-62.1	-67.3	-71.9	-76.6	-80.8	-85.2	-89.9	-92.6	-295.3	-720.4
PEP and Pease	-5.5	-12.0	-13.6	-15.0	-16.4	-17.6	-18.9	-20.2	-21.5	-22.2	-62.5	-162.9
Lower Rate on Capital Gains and Dividends	-13.0	-11.9	-30.3	-31.9	-33.7	-35.3	-35.8	-38.2	-39.9	-41.1	-120.8	-311.1
Other Provisions	-0.1	-0.3	-0.3	-0.3	-0.3	-0.3	-0.2	-0.2	-0.2	-0.2	-1.3	-2.4
Total	-102.7	-203.4	-229.5	-238.7	-247.3	-255.4	-261.9	-270.5	-278.7	-287.1	-1,021.6	-2,375.2
Debt service	-1.0	-4.5	-9.6	-21.4	-35.1	-48.7	-62.4	-76.0	-89.5	-102.5	-71.6	-450.7
Total plus AMT indexed for inflation with debt service	-233.3	-311.0	-356.5	-397.6	-443.3	-493.6	-544.5	-600.0	-659.6	-721.7	-1,741.7	-4,761.1

Source: Joint Committee on Taxation, Congressional Budget Office, and CRS calculations (FY2022).

Table 2. Percentage Change in After-Tax Income Due to Bush Tax Cut Provisions, by Income Category

Income Category	Reduced Tax Rates: 10%, 25%, 28%	Reduced Tax Rates: 33%, 35%	Repeal PEP/Pease	Reduced Capital Gains Tax Rate	Reduced Dividends Tax Rate	Reduced Marriage Penalty	Expanded Tax Credits	Average After-Tax Income
Poorest Quintile	0.1	0.0	0.0	0.0	0.0	0.2	0.9	$10,702
Quintile 2	1.0	0.0	0.0	0.0	0.0	0.3	1.3	$23,359
Quintile 3	1.3	0.0	0.0	0.1	0.0	0.1	0.7	$38,362
Quintile 4	1.3	0.0	0.0	0.1	0.0	0.4	0.4	$61,176
80-90 percentile	1.6	0.0	0.0	0.1	0.1	0.7	0.1	$88,999
90-95 percentile	1.8	0.0	0.0	0.2	0.1	0.5	0.0	$124,146
95-99 percentile	1.5	0.1	0.3	0.4	0.2	0.3	0.0	$213,506
Richest 1%	0.3	1.9	0.9	1.3	0.8	0.1	0.0	$1,071,100
All	1.2	0.3	0.2	0.3	0.2	0.3	0.3	$58,277
Suits index	0.0895	-0.7979	-0.7325	-0.5768	-0.6641	0.1048	0.6733	

Source: CRS analysis of Tax Policy Center estimates.

OPTIONS REGARDING THE BUSH TAX CUTS

There are several options that Congress may consider regarding the Bush tax cuts. The two extreme options have been discussed along the following lines. Allowing the Bush tax cuts to expire as scheduled will somewhat improve the fiscal condition, but could stifle the economic recovery. At the other extreme, permanently extending all of the Bush tax cuts would not undercut the economic recovery, but would worsen the longer-term fiscal outlook and possibly signal a lack of progress in dealing with the long-term fiscal situation. In either case, the United States is facing increasing budget deficits and federal debt levels over the long term.

The Obama Administration has proposed to allow the Bush tax cuts to expire at the end of 2012 for high-income taxpayers (single taxpayers with income more than $200,000 and married taxpayers with income more than $250,000—the richest 2% of taxpayers) and permanently extend the tax cuts for other taxpayers (the middle-income tax cuts). The specific proposals are to reinstate the 39.6% tax rate, reinstate the 36% tax rate for high-income taxpayers, reinstate PEP and Pease for high-income taxpayers, and increase the long-term capital gains and qualified dividend tax rate to 20% for high-income taxpayers. Compared with permanently extending all of the Bush tax cuts (with more than $7,000 billion in total deficits), this proposal is projected to increase tax revenues by $312 billion over five years and by $789 billion over 10 years (see **Table 3**). The 10-year reduction in estimated debt service is $140 billion. In total, this proposal could reduce budget deficits by $931 billion over 10 years.

Some policy makers and analysts have proposed alternative income thresholds to define high-income taxpayers. The thresholds that have frequently been discussed are $500,000 and $1 million for both single and joint taxpayers. The revenue gains (and associated debt service reductions) from allowing the Bush tax cuts to expire for high-income taxpayers with income over the two alternative thresholds are reported in **Table 3**. The estimated 10-year revenue gain under the $500,000 income threshold is $566 billion—about 72% of the revenue gain under the Obama Administration proposal. The estimated revenue gain falls as the income threshold rises so that a $1 million income threshold to define high-income taxpayers is estimated to raise $401 billion over 10 years—about 51% of the revenue gain under the Obama Administration proposal.

Extending the Bush tax cuts will almost double the 10-year total deficit from CBO's baseline projection (the projected total deficit would be much higher if the AMT were also indexed for inflation). These options could help reduce the total projected deficit, but only by 7% to 13% depending on the option.

LONG-TERM ECONOMIC EFFECTS OF TAX RATE INCREASES

It is often argued that increasing tax rates will reduce consumer spending in the short term, and work effort, saving, and investment—all key components of economic growth—in the long term. In an underemployed economy, short-term spending increases and tax cuts—expansionary fiscal policies—are expected to facilitate job creation, reduce unemployment, and increase output; spending cuts and tax hikes—contractionary fiscal policies—

Table 3. Revenue Gain and Deficit Reduction from Expiration of Bush Tax Cuts for High-Income Taxpayers (billions of dollars)

	2013	2014	2015	2016	2017	2018	2019	2020	2021	2022	2013-2017	2013-2022
A. Single: $200,000/Joint: $250,000												
Revenue Gain	33.9	52.1	69.2	75.5	80.8	85.9	90.1	95.5	100.7	104.1	311.6	787.8
Debt Service	0.3	1.3	2.8	6.3	10.6	15.0	19.6	24.3	29.1	33.8	21.3	143.1
Deficit Reduction	34.2	53.4	72.0	81.8	91.4	100.9	109.7	119.8	129.8	137.9	332.9	930.9
B. Single and Joint: $500,000												
Revenue Gain	23.8	36.1	49.9	54.5	58.3	61.9	64.8	68.7	72.4	74.9	222.7	565.5
Debt Service	0.2	0.9	1.9	4.5	7.6	10.7	14.0	17.4	20.9	24.3	15.1	102.4
Deficit Reduction	24.0	37.0	51.8	59.0	65.9	72.6	78.8	86.1	93.3	99.2	237.8	667.9
C. Single and Joint: $1million												
Revenue Gain	16.3	24.5	35.5	38.9	41.6	44.1	46.1	48.9	51.5	53.3	156.8	400.6
Debt Service	0.2	0.6	1.3	3.1	5.3	7.6	9.9	12.3	14.8	17.2	10.5	72.3
Deficit Reduction	16.5	25.1	36.8	42.0	46.9	51.7	56.0	61.2	66.3	70.5	167.3	472.9

Source: CRS estimates and calculations.

Notes: Baseline is the permanent extension of the Bush tax cuts provisions; interactions with AMT are not included in estimates.

are expected to have the opposite effect.[15] The main argument against allowing the Bush tax cuts to expire at the end of 2010 was the weak recovery and the fear of pushing the economy back into recession, an argument likely to be made in 2012. These short-term effects operate through the demand-side of the economy.

Some argue that tax increases reduce economic growth and kill jobs. However, once the economy has recovered from the recession and is back to full employment, long-term economic growth is a supply-side phenomenon and is facilitated by increasing work effort, saving, and investment. Economic research suggests that modest tax rate increases would have little negative impact on long-term economic growth and job creation. In the long run, the market economy naturally generates jobs; consequently, there is little need to use fiscal policy to address job creation.[16]

Work Effort

For most taxpayers, the majority of income is from labor earnings or wages. Income taxes affect after-tax incomes and after-tax wages. A rise in the tax rate will reduce after-tax wages and, it is argued, work effort (i.e., labor supply). Economic theory suggests that the effect of earnings changes on labor supply is ambiguous. An earnings decrease has a price effect (substitution effect) and an income effect, which sum to the total effect. Earnings can be thought of as the price of leisure (i.e., what is given up to increase leisure). If the price of leisure falls (due to a tax rate increase, for example), then an individual will purchase more leisure (i.e., work less), holding income constant. But if earnings fall then income also falls. This, by itself, leads an individual to purchase less of all normal goods including leisure. The substitution and income effects thus work in opposite directions. Without additional information, the total effect cannot be determined. A large empirical literature, however, shows that men's labor supply is insensitive to changes in wages.[17] In addition, a body of empirical work also suggests that men's labor is insensitive to changes in tax rates.[18] Research shows that even the labor supply of high-income men is insensitive to changes in tax rates.[19]

It has been argued that taxes can affect a married woman's labor supply directly by changing her after-tax wages and indirectly by changing her husband's after-tax wages. Early evidence showed that women's labor supply was more sensitive to wages than men's. Recent evidence, however, shows that married women's labor supply after 1990 was considerably less sensitive to their own wages and their husband's wages than before 1990—women's labor supply decisions were becoming more like men's.[20]

While income from labor supply may not be sensitive to taxes, taxable income may be sensitive to tax changes. Taxpayers may be able to reduce taxable income by taking more deductions, deferring compensation, excluding income by contributing more to individual retirement accounts and 401(k) plans, or taking income in another form (e.g., as capital gains instead of earnings). High-income taxpayers typically have more opportunity to respond to tax changes and reduce taxable income through these methods.

Several studies have investigated the sensitivity of taxable income to tax rates. Most studies find that taxable income is more responsive to tax rate changes than labor supply, though the empirical estimates suggest that a 10% increase in tax rates could reduce taxable income by 1.2% to 4%.[21] Furthermore, a reduction in taxable income may not be a complete loss to the economy or tax revenues. If high-income taxpayers react to higher individual income tax rates by saving more in a 401(k) plan or shifting income to the corporate form, this income will be taxed in the future (in the case of the 401(k) plan) or taxed under the corporate income tax.

Saving and Investment

The long-run level of output depends on the amount of saving and investment. Saving and investment increase the amount of capital in the economy and hence, aggregate supply (i.e., the amount of goods and services available in the economy). National saving is made up of saving by the government (public saving) and by households and firms (private saving). Public saving is equal to the government's deficit or surplus—it is negative for a deficit and positive for a surplus. It is national saving that affects the long-run level of output. Many argue that increasing tax rates, especially the tax rate on capital gains, will reduce saving and, hence, long-term economic growth.[22]

Households save by investing in their own business or investing in equities, bonds, and other financial instruments. Changing capital gains tax rates changes the after-tax rate of return on investments (e.g., reducing the tax rate increases the after-tax return). The change in the rate of return has two offsetting effects on saving. Increasing the rate of return can increase households' willingness to save (the substitution effect). But at the same time, the increased return allows households to save less to maintain their desired or target wealth level (the income effect).

About half of equity income is in tax-preferred savings accounts such as 401(k) pension plans and individual retirement accounts. Additionally, capital gains are only taxed when realized, and a substantial portion are never realized. Consequently, the effect of capital gains tax changes on private saving is likely to be small.

The traditional economic theory of saving, the life-cycle model, assumes that individuals make rational, far-sighted decisions. The preponderance of empirical evidence, however, does not support the life-cycle model.[23] Behavioral theories of saving emphasize the role of inertia, the lack of self-control, and the limit of human intellectual capabilities. To cope with the complexities involved in making saving decisions, individuals often use simple rules of thumb and develop target levels of wealth. Once their target level of wealth is obtained, many individuals suspend active saving.[24] Saving rates have fallen over the past 30 years while the capital gains tax rate has fallen from 28% in 1987 to 15% today (0% for taxpayers in the 10% and 15% tax brackets). This suggests that changing capital gains tax rates have had little effect on private saving.

Capital gains tax rate increases appear to increase public saving and may have little or no effect on private saving. Consequently, a capital gains tax increase could have a positive overall impact on national saving.

CONCLUDING REMARKS

The 2012 debate over the fate of the Bush tax cuts is likely to take place in an almost as bleak economic and fiscal environment as the 2010 debate over the fate of the Bush tax cuts. In the short term, the economy is growing slowly and unemployment is likely to remain over 8.5% for several more months. The long-term federal government fiscal situation is clearly unsustainable. The decision over the fate of the Bush tax cuts will affect the short-term economic situation and the long-term fiscal situation. The options will likely range from allowing all of the Bush tax cuts to expire after 2012 to temporarily or permanently extending some or all of the Bush tax cuts. It can be argued that permanently extending all of the Bush tax cuts could make future tax reforms to deal with unsustainable deficits and debt trends more difficult. If the economy is still weak, a temporary extension would not harm the economy. Furthermore, allowing the high-income tax cuts to expire as scheduled could help reduce budget deficits in the short term without stifling the economic recovery.[25] Research has shown that tax cuts directed to high-income taxpayers have a small stimulative effect because they tend to save any additional income.[26] Increasing tax rates for the richest 1% to 3% of taxpayers (by allowing the high-income tax cuts to expire) would likely neither significantly decrease consumer expenditures nor adversely affect short-term job growth.[27] Increasing taxes to reduce long-term budget deficits after the economy has recovered, would likely have little negative impact on long-term economic growth and job creation.

APPENDIX. THE SUITS INDEX

The progressivity measure used is a modified Suits index. The Suits index was originally developed to measure the progressivity of the tax burden.[28] Since benefits from tax provisions are considered, the modified Suits index is the negative of the original Suits index.

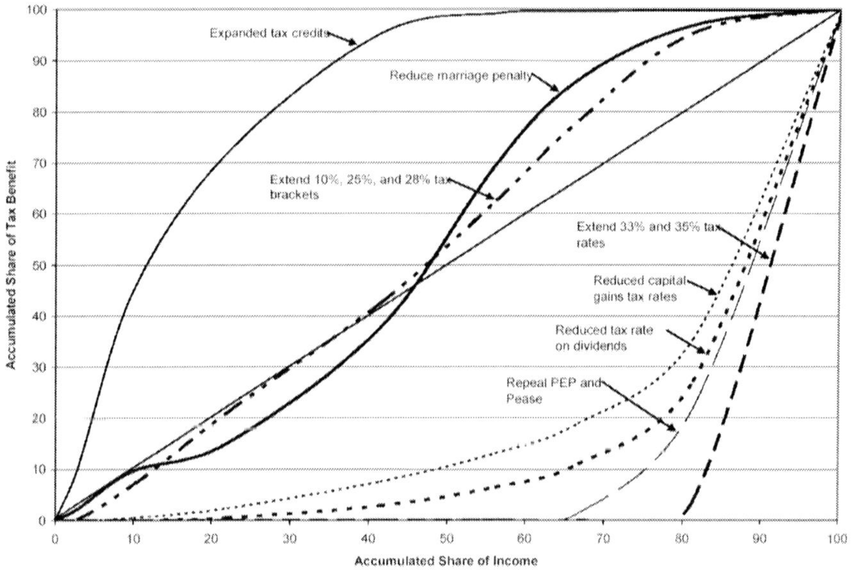

Source: CRS analysis of Tax Policy Center estimates.

Figure A-1. Lorenz Curves of Bush Tax Cut Provisions, 2012.

The index is based on the Lorenz curve. **Figure A-1** displays the Lorenz curves for the seven tax provisions making up the Bush tax cuts that are considered in this study. The horizontal axis is the accumulated share of income when tax units are ranked by income from lowest to highest. The vertical axis is the accumulated share of tax benefits from the tax provisions. The diagonal line is the Lorenz curve for a proportionally distributed tax benefit. A progressive benefit will have its Lorenz curve above the diagonal line (e.g., see the Lorenz curve for expanded tax credits). This means that tax units with lower incomes receive benefits that are a larger proportion of their income than higher income tax units. Conversely, a regressive benefit (e.g., the repeal of PEP and Pease) will have a Lorenz curve below the diagonal line.

Let the area under the Lorenz curve be denoted as L—it is the area bounded from below by the horizontal axis and from above by the Lorenz curve. Let the area under the diagonal line be denoted as K. The Suits index, S, is therefore defined as:

$$S = \frac{L - K}{K}.$$

End Notes

[1] Joint Committee on Taxation, *Estimated Budget Effects of the "Tax Relief, Unemployment Insurance Reauthorization, and Job Creation Act of 2010," Scheduled for Consideration by the United States Senate*, JCX-54-10, December 10, 2010.

[2] *Blue Chip Economic Indicators*, vol. 37, no. 7 (July 10, 2012).

[3] Carmen M. Reinhart and Vincent R. Reinhart, "After the Fall," presented at the Federal Reserve Bank of Kansas City Jackson Hole Symposium, Jackson, WY, August 26-28, 2010.

[4] CBO, *The Budget and Economic Outlook: Fiscal Years 2002-2011*, January 2001.

[5] CBO, *The Budget and Economic Outlook: Fiscal Years 2008 to 2018*, January 2008.

[6] The Tax Policy Center estimates that 28.5 million taxpayers would be subject to the AMT without the annual AMT fix. In 2009, 4 million taxpayers were subject to the AMT. See Tax Policy Center, *Aggregate AMT Projections, 2009-2020*, Table T10-0106, May 3, 2010.

[7] CBO, *CBO's 2011 Long-Term Budget Outlook*, June 2011, table 1.1 for assumptions about spending and revenues under each scenario.

[8] CBO, CBO's 2011 Long-Term Budget Outlook, June 2011, p. 31.

[9] For more information, see CRS Report R41796, *Deficit Reduction: The Economic and Tax Revenue Effects of Personal Exemption Phaseout (PEP) and Limitation on Itemized Deductions (Pease)*, by Thomas L. Hungerford.

[10] For more information, see CRS Report R40411, *The Economic Effects of Capital Gains Taxation*, by Thomas L. Hungerford.

[11] For more information, see CRS Report R41999, *The Impact of Refundable Tax Credits on Poverty Rates*, by Margot L. Crandall-Hollick.

[12] The estimates were prepared by the Urban-Brookings Tax Policy Center.

[13] See the Appendix for more details on the Suits index.

[14] Thomas L. Hungerford, "The Redistributive Effect of Selected Federal Transfer and Tax Provisions," *Public Finance Review*, vol. 38, no. 4 (July 2010), pp. 450-472.

[15] CRS Report R41849, *Can Contractionary Fiscal Policy Be Expansionary?*, by Jane G. Gravelle and Thomas L. Hungerford.

[16] CRS Report R41392, *Small Business and the Expiration of the 2001 Tax Rate Reductions: Economic Issues*, by Jane G. Gravelle.

[17] This literature is reviewed in Mark Killingsworth, *Labor Supply* (Cambridge: Cambridge University Press, 1983).

[18] This literature is reviewed in Jerry R. Hausman, "Taxes and Labor Supply," in *Handbook of Public Economics*, eds. Alan J. Auerbach and Martin Feldstein, vol. 1 (Amsterdam: North-Holland, 1985), pp. 213-263.

[19] Robert A. Moffit and Mark O. Wilhelm, "Taxation and the Labor Supply Decisions of the Affluent," in *Does Atlas Shrug?*, ed. Joel B. Slemrod (Cambridge, MA: Harvard University Press, 2000), pp. 193-239.

[20] Francine D. Blau and Lawrence M. Kahn, "Changes in the Labor Supply Behavior of Married Women: 1980-2000," *Journal of Labor Economics*, vol. 25, no. 3 (2007), pp. 393-438; and Bradley T. Heim, "The Incredible Shrinking Elasticities: Married Female Labor Supply, 1978-2002," *Journal of Human Resources*, vol. 42, no. 4 (Fall 2007), pp. 881-918.

[21] See Emmanuel Saez, Joel B. Slemrod, and Seth H. Giertz, "The Elasticity of Taxable Income with Respect to Marginal Tax Rates: A Critical Review," *Journal of Economic Literature*, forthcoming available at http://elsa.berkeley.edu/~saez/saez-slemrod-giertzJEL10final.pdf.

[22] For more information on capital gains taxes, see CRS Report R40411, *The Economic Effects of Capital Gains Taxation*, by Thomas L. Hungerford.

[23] For a discussion and citations to the literature see CRS Report RL33482, *Saving Incentives: What May Work, What May Not*, by Thomas L. Hungerford.

[24] F. Thomas Juster, Joseph P. Lupton, James P. Smith, and Frank Stafford, "The Decline in Household Saving and the Wealth Effect," *Review of Economics and Statistics*, vol. 87, no. 4 (November 2005), pp. 20-27.

[25] Tax cuts to the wealthy tend to be saved rather than spent and have little impact on short-term economic growth. See CRS Report R40104, *Economic Stimulus: Issues and Policies*, by Jane G. Gravelle, Thomas L. Hungerford, and Marc Labonte.

[26] See CRS Report R40104, *Economic Stimulus: Issues and Policies*, by Jane G. Gravelle, Thomas L. Hungerford, and Marc Labonte.

[27] See CRS Report R41392, *Small Business and the Expiration of the 2001 Tax Rate Reductions: Economic Issues*, by Jane G. Gravelle.

[28] Daniel B. Suits, "Measurement of Tax Progressivity," *American Economic Review*, vol. 67, no. 4 (September 1977), pp. 747-752.

In: Tax Rates
Editor: Howard P. Durham

ISBN: 978-1-62417-215-1

Chapter 5

THE ECONOMIC EFFECTS OF CAPITAL GAINS TAXATION*

Thomas L. Hungerford

SUMMARY

One provision of the 1913 individual income tax that generated a great deal of confusion was the taxation of income from the sale of property (i.e., capital gains income). This initial confusion has led to almost 100 years of legislative debates over capital gains. Beginning in 1922 capital gains were first subject to lower tax rates than ordinary income. This preferential treatment has continued throughout most of the history of the income tax. Proposals dealing with the taxation of capital gains have ranged from the outright elimination of capital gains taxation to the reduction of capital gains tax rates for certain classes of taxpayers to the elimination of the preferential tax treatment.

Overall, capital gains tax revenues have been a fairly small, but not trivial, source of government revenue. Since 1954, revenue from the capital gains tax as a share of total income tax revenue has averaged 5.2%. It reached a peak of 12.8% in 1986 and a low of 2.0% in 1957. Nonetheless, the 2007 capital gains tax revenue of $123 billion was equal to 75% of the FY2007 budget deficit.

* This is an edited, reformatted and augmented version of a Congressional Research Services publication,dated June 18, 2010.

Some argue that reducing capital gains tax rates will increase tax revenues by dramatically increasing capital gains realizations. While the effect of changes in the capital gains tax rate continue to be debated and researched, the bulk of the evidence suggests that reducing the capital gains tax rate reduces tax revenues.

Higher income households are substantially more likely to own assets that can generate taxable gains than lower income households. Additionally, high income households own most of these assets, realize most of the capital gains, and pay most of the capital gains taxes at preferential rates.

Capital gains tax reductions are often proposed as a policy that will increase saving and investment, provide a short-term economic stimulus, and boost long-term economic growth. Capital gains tax rate reductions appear to decrease public saving and may have little or no effect on private saving. Consequently, many analysts note that capital gains tax reductions likely have a negative overall impact on national saving. Furthermore, capital gains tax rate reductions, they observe, are unlikely to have much effect on the long-term level of output or the path to the long-run level of output (i.e., economic growth). A tax reduction on capital gains would mostly benefit very high income taxpayers who are likely to save most of any tax reduction. A temporary capital gains tax reduction possibly could have a negative impact on short-term economic growth.

INTRODUCTION

One provision of the 1913 individual income tax that generated a great deal of confusion was the taxation of income from the sale of property (i.e., capital gains income). This initial confusion has led to almost 100 years of legislative debates over capital gains. For the first nine years of the individual income tax, capital gains received no preferential treatment and were taxed as ordinary income. Beginning in 1922, however, capital gains were first subject to lower tax rates than ordinary income. This preferential treatment has continued throughout most of the history of the income tax.

Proposals and legislation dealing with the taxation of capital gains have ranged from the outright elimination of capital gains taxation to the reduction of capital gains tax rates for certain classes of taxpayers to the elimination of the preferential tax treatment. For example, the American Recovery and Reinvestment Act of 2009 (ARRA; P.L. 111-5) increased the exclusion of capital gains from the sale of certain small business stock held for more than five years from 50% to 75%.

How Capital Gains Are Taxed

Proposals to deal with how capital gains are taxed depend on how capital gains are defined. Under the Haig-Simons approach, income is defined as consumption plus the change in wealth.[1] Wealth can increase because of active saving or because the value of assets has increased; capital gains are the increase in the value of capital assets. Under this income definition, real or inflation-adjusted capital gains would be taxed each year as they accrue and real capital losses would be deducted. It has long been recognized, however, that taxing real capital gains as they accrue may be impractical especially for capital assets that are not actively traded.

Given the difficulties of taxing capital gains as they accrue, capital gains are taxed as they are realized (that is, when the capital asset is sold or exchanged). Capital assets are property, but there are exceptions such as business inventory, accounts receivable acquired in the ordinary course of business, copyrights, and literary compositions.[2] Capital gains are calculated by subtracting the asset's basis from the sales price. An asset's basis is the original purchase price adjusted for certain additions and deductions; it is not adjusted for inflation. If the basis is greater than the sales price then it is a capital loss.

Capital gains are taxed at various rates. For the 2008 tax year, short-term capital gains (gains on capital assets held for less than one year) are taxed as ordinary income. Long-term capital gains are taxed at a 0% tax rate for taxpayers in the two lowest tax brackets (the 10% and 15% tax brackets) and at 15% for other taxpayers. Capital gains and capital losses are treated asymmetrically. Capital losses are subtracted from capital gains before calculating tax liability. If capital losses exceed capital gains, then up to $3,000 of capital losses can be deducted from ordinary income. Capital losses in excess of $3,000 can be carried over and subtracted from income in future years.[3]

Capital Gains Tax Rates and Tax Revenues

Both capital gains tax rates and tax revenues have constantly changed since the establishment of the income tax. Tax revenues depend on the tax rate and capital gains realizations. Capital gains realizations, in turn, depend on tax rates as well as other factors.

Tax Rates

Throughout most of the history of the income tax, the maximum capital gains tax rate has been lower than the maximum tax rate on ordinary income. Figure 1 displays the capital gains and ordinary income tax rates for the past 50 years. With the exception of a three-year period (1988- 1990), the capital gains tax rate was considerably below the tax rate for ordinary income. After 2010, the capital gains tax rate is scheduled to revert back to 20%. The 15% maximum capital gains tax rate between 2003 and 2010 is the lowest rate on long-term capital gains since the Second World War.

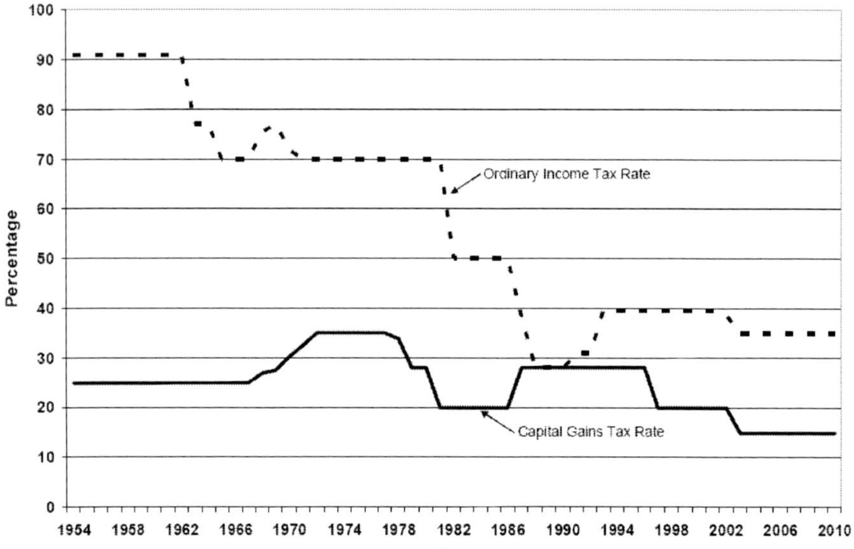

Source: Department of the Treasury.

Figure 1. Maximum Tax Rates on Capital Gains and Ordinary Income, 1954-2010.

Tax Revenues

Overall, capital gains tax revenues have been a fairly small, but not trivial, source of government revenue. Since 1954, revenue from the capital gains tax as a share of total income tax revenue has averaged 5.2%. It reached a peak of 12.8% in 1986 and a low of 2.0% in 1957. Nonetheless, the 2007 capital gains tax revenue of $123 billion was equal to 75% of the FY2007 budget deficit.

Capital gains tax revenue generally follows the same trend as capital gains realizations. Figure 2 shows both as a percentage of gross domestic product (GDP) from 1954 to 2008 along with CBO projections to 2019. Realizations and revenues hit peaks in 1986, 2000, and 2007.

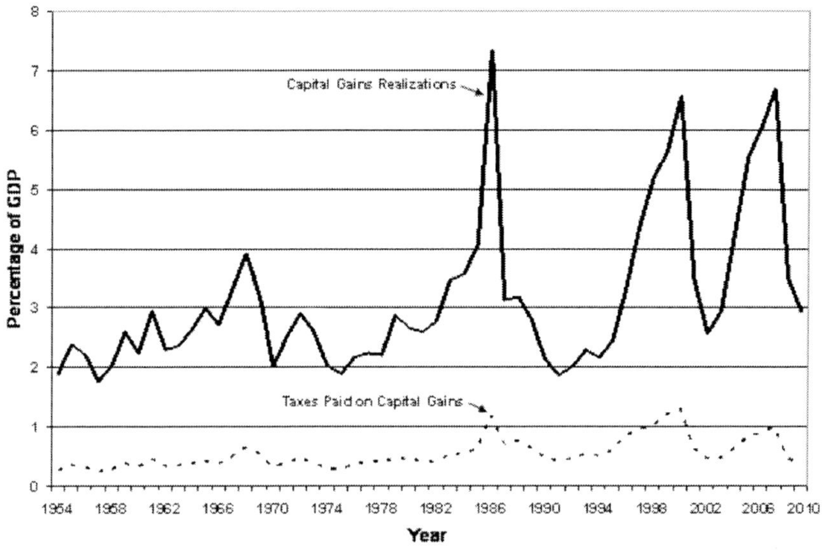

Figure 2. Capital Gains Realizations and Tax Revenue, 1954-2010; (As a percentage of GDP) Source: Department of the Treasury and CBO.

Behavioral Responses to Capital Gains Tax Rate Changes

The capital gains tax discourages capital gains realizations because capital gains are only taxed when realized. Consequently, taxpayers tend to hold on to appreciated assets they would otherwise sell. Furthermore, step-up in basis at death gives taxpayers an incentive to hold assets until death and pass them to their heirs. In these ways, the capital gains tax is said to produce a "lock-in" effect. This effect imposes efficiency losses because investors may be encouraged to hold suboptimal portfolios or forego investment opportunities with higher pre-tax returns. Changes in the capital gains tax rate can exacerbate or reduce lock-in effects, and thus affect realizations and tax revenues.

Changes in the capital gains tax rate tend to track capital gains realizations. Figure 3 shows the maximum capital gains tax rate and capital gains realizations as a percentage of GDP. The major spikes in realizations correspond to changes in the tax rate. The simple correlation between the two time-series is -0.64, which suggests that realizations increase when the tax rate decreases. It is this relationship that has led some to argue that decreasing the capital gains tax rate will increase capital gains tax revenues.

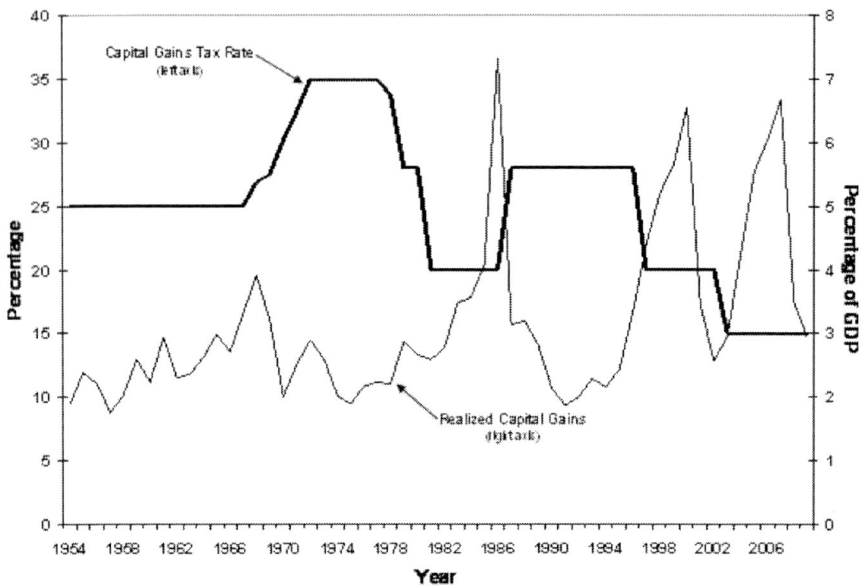

Source: Department of the Treasury.

Figure 3. Capital Gains Tax Rates and Realizations, 1954-2009.

An early study by Martin Feldstein, Joel Slemrod, and Shlomo Yitzhaki examined capital gains realizations and concluded that "reducing the tax on capital gains would not only encourage a more active market in corporate stock but would also increase tax revenue."[4] Their estimated elasticity was about 3.8, suggesting that a 10% reduction in the tax rate would increase realizations by 38%. This estimate was criticized because it used data from only one year—1973.[5] This cross-sectional evidence was likely picking up a temporary timing response in realizations from the tax rate change rather than a behavioral response to a permanent change in the tax rate.[6]

Some analysts have argued that a large permanent response to capital gains tax rate changes is implausible. Alan Auerbach has suggested that there is nothing in the historical record of capital gains to justify a large elasticity.[7] Jane Gravelle points out that capital gains realizations cannot be greater than accruals. Her simulation model suggests an upper limit for the permanent realization elasticity is 0.5.[8]

Empirical research has tried to separate the transitory response from the permanent response. Gerald Auten and Charles Clotfelter used panel data, a dataset containing observations on individuals over a period of years (1969 to 1973), to estimate the temporary and permanent effects of a capital gains tax cut.[9] They estimate a transitory elasticity that is generally greater than 1.0 (the simple average from all their specifications is 1.5) suggesting that a 10% reduction in the tax rate would lead to a 15% increase in short-run realizations (the timing response). The permanent or long-run elasticity they estimated was 0.5.

In subsequent research, Leonard Burman and William Randolph estimate a permanent elasticity that is closer to zero than to 0.5.[10] They, however, report a large transitory elasticity of 6.4. A large transitory elasticity and a low permanent elasticity are consistent with the pattern of capital gains realizations shown in Figure 3. Changes in the tax rate or anticipated changes have coincided with large increases in capital gains realizations, but realizations quickly fell back to previous levels. The spike in 1986 was due to the transitory response to the announced increase in the capital gains tax rate to take effect in 1987. The spikes in 2000 and 2007 were the transitory responses to capital gains tax rate reductions.

Over the years, a variety of studies have estimated different long-run or permanent realizations elasticities. The general trend has been to estimate elasticities closer to zero than to 1.0 as data and estimation methods improve, though there are exceptions. However, even an elasticity of 1.0 does not mean that reducing the capital gains tax rate is revenue neutral. Taxpayers may increase their capital gains realizations by shifting other income into capital gains. This may increase capital gains tax revenue, but will reduce tax revenues from other sources—overall, tax revenues fall. While the effect of changes in the capital gains tax rate continue to be debated and researched, the bulk of the evidence suggests that reducing the capital gains tax rate reduces tax revenues.

DISTRIBUTIONAL ISSUES

Three questions can be asked about distributional issues related to capital gains: (1) who owns the assets that can generate capital gains? (2) who realizes capital gains? and (3) who pays capital gains taxes? Each question is examined. Two data sources are used for the analysis: the Federal Reserve Board's 2007 Survey of Consumer Finances (SCF) and the IRS's 2004 Statistics of Income Public Use File (SOI PUF). See the Appendix for a description of each data source.

Assets and Accrued Capital Gains

Most assets owned by households would not be subject to capital gains taxes when sold. Figure 4 reports the various assets that households owned in 2007. Over half of the total is accounted for by retirement accounts (e.g., 401(k)s and IRAs) and principal residences. Retirement accounts generally are not taxed until the funds are withdrawn at retirement. At that time, the withdrawals are taxed as ordinary income. Up to $500,000 of the gain from the sale of a principal residence can be excluded from income taxes. Farm and business assets and other real estate (e.g., rental property, and vacation homes) account for 33% of household assets. The final 13% of household assets are financial assets (i.e., stocks, bonds, and mutual funds).

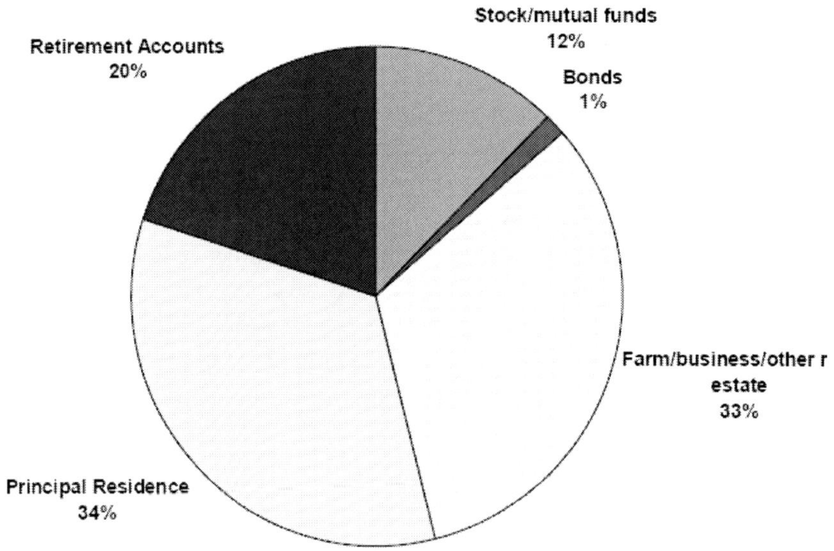

Source: CRS analysis of the 2007 SCF.

Figure 4. Assets Owned by Households, 2007.

Higher income households are more likely to own assets that can generate taxable capital gains than lower income households. Table 1 reports the proportion of households in each income category owning particular assets. For each type of asset, the proportion owning increases as income increases. For example, 7% of the poorest 20% of households own stocks or mutual funds compared to 72% of the richest 5% of households.

Table 1. Percentage Owning Assets by Income, 2007

Income category	Stocks/mutual funds	Bonds	Farm, business, other	Principal residence	Retirement accounts
Quintile 1	6.9%	0.3%	10.0%	40.5%	11.2%
Quintile 2	11.5	0.2	13.5	57.1	34.6
Quintile 3	20.5	1.1	24.2	72.5	56.9
Quintile 4	30.4	1.2	31.0	82.6	73.6
Quintile 5	52.2	5.4	51.7	90.7	87.1
Top 10%	59.9	9.3	64.6	92.6	89.8
Top 5%	71.9	13.7	75.7	93.8	91.4

Source: CRS analysis of the 2007 SCF.

Most of the assets are owned by higher income households. Well over half of the assets that can generate taxable capital gains are owned by the richest 5% of households (see **Table 2**). Principal residences are more broadly distributed in the income distribution than other assets, but most of the gains from the sale of homes is excluded from federal taxation.

Table 2. Distribution of Assets by Income, 2007

Income category	Stocks/mutual funds	Bonds	Farm, business, other	Principal residence	Retirement Accounts
Quintile 1	1.0%	0.7%	3.1%	4.9%	0.4%
Quintile 2	1.5	0.2	3.0	9.1	2.4
Quintile 3	4.2	2.0	5.1	15.0	7.0
Quintile 4	10.2	3.8	9.5	22.0	20.4
Quintile 5	83.0	93.3	79.2	49.1	69.8
Top 10%	75.9	89.5	71.3	33.1	51.3
Top 5%	66.4	85.5	60.8	22.3	37.4

Source: CRS analysis of the 2007 SCF.

The distribution of capital accruals tends to follow the same pattern as the distribution of asset ownership. Table 3 reports the distribution of accrued capital gains for selected assets.[11] Capital gains accruals for stocks, mutual funds, and businesses are highly skewed toward the upper income levels. About 90% of capital gains accruals go to households in the richest income quintile and 70% go to the richest 5% of households. Capital gains accruals on principal residences, however, are less skewed—only 47% go to households in the richest income quintile.

Table 3. Accrued Capital Gains by Income, 2007

Income category	Stocks/mutual funds	Businesses	Other real estate	Principal residences
Quintile 1	0.7%	1.8%	3.3%	5.5%
Quintile 2	0.6	2.0	4.1	9.9
Quintile 3	1.5	2.8	8.2	16.0
Quintile 4	7.0	5.6	14.0	21.2
Quintile 5	90.2	87.8	70.4	47.4
Top 10%	85.4	80.6	60.0	31.6
Top 5%	75.7	69.2	49.4	20.9

Source: CRS analysis of the 2007 SCF.

Capital Gains Realizations and Taxes

The distribution of realized capital gains can be examined by one of two methods. First, the focus can be on how capital gains are distributed among all households. This allows for an examination of how income from capital gains is distributed throughout the entire income distribution.

Second, the focus can be narrowed to examine how realized capital gains are distributed among taxpayers—the group that reports income from capital gains. Many lower income individuals and families, such as those with income primarily from public assistance or Social Security, do not file tax returns and would be excluded from the analysis. Both methods are employed.

Income from realized capital gains, while always concentrated at the top of the income distribution, has become more concentrated over the past 25 years. Figure 5 displays the distribution of realized capital gains among all households (whether or not they filed tax returns) since 1979. In 1979, households in the bottom 95% of the income distribution received about 20% of total capital gains income (the dark grey and white bars). The richest 0.1% of households (about 81,000 households) received 36% of total capital gains income. By 2005, the bottom 95% received only 10% of total capital gains income while the richest 0.1% (about 114,000 households) received 50%.

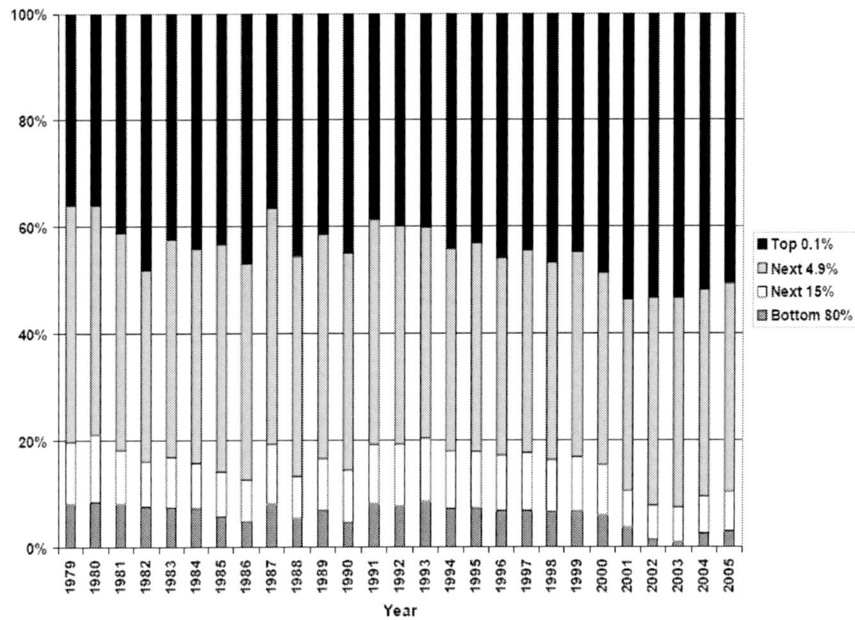

Source: CBO, Historical Effective Tax Rates, 1979-2005: Supplement, December 2008.

Figure 5. Distribution of Realized Capital Gains by Income, 1979-2005.

Income from realized capital gains is only slightly more broadly distributed among taxpayers. Table 4 reports the distribution of long-term capital gains and all capital gains in 2004. Longterm capital gains are taxed at preferential rates while short-term capital gains are not. About 18% of total long-term capital gains were received by taxpayers in the bottom 80% of the income distribution. Taxpayers in the top 20% received about 82% of total long-term capital gains and taxpayers in the richest 5% received 68% of total capital gains in 2004.

Table 4. Capital Gains Income and Capital Gains Taxes, 2004

Income category	Long-term capital gains	All capital gains	Taxes paid on capital gains
Quintile 1	2.7%	2.8%	1.4%
Quintile 2	3.3	3.5	2.1
Quintile 3	5.2	5.4	3.7
Quintile 4	6.9	7.0	6.1
Quintile 5	81.9	81.3	86.7
Top 10%	74.6	74.2	79.2
Top 5%	68.2	67.5	71.7

Source: 2004 IRS SOI PUF.

The final column of Table 4 reports the distribution of capital gains taxes (on both short-term and long-term capital gains). Overall, the distributional pattern is similar to the capital gains income distribution, but slightly more skewed toward the higher income levels. The primary reason is that lower income taxpayers faced a 5% long-term capital gains tax rate in 2004 while higher income taxpayers faced a 15% tax rate.

ECONOMIC ISSUES

Capital gains tax reductions are often proposed as a policy that will increase saving and investment, provide a short-term economic stimulus, and boost long-term economic growth. Each of these arguments is examined.

Saving and Investment

National saving is made up of saving by the government (public saving) and by households and firms (private saving). Public saving is equal to the government's deficit or surplus—it is negative for a deficit and positive for a surplus. Reducing capital gains tax rates will likely reduce public saving because it reduces tax revenues without affecting outlays; this increases a budget deficit or decreases a budget surplus.[12]

Households save by investing in their own business or investing in stocks, bonds, and other financial instruments. Changing capital gains tax rates changes the after-tax rate of return on investments (for example, reducing the tax rate increases the after-tax return). The change in the rate of return has two offsetting effects on saving. Increasing the rate of return can increase households' willingness to save (the substitution effect). But at the same time, the increased return allows households to save less to maintain their desired or target wealth level (the income effect). Consequently, the effect of capital gains taxes on private saving is likely to be small.

The traditional economic theory of saving, the life-cycle model, assumes that individuals make rational, far-sighted decisions. The preponderance of empirical evidence, however, does not support the life-cycle model.[13] Behavioral theories of saving emphasize the role of inertia, the lack of self-control, and the limit of human intellectual capabilities. To cope with the complexities involved in making saving decisions, individuals often use simple rules of thumb and develop target levels of wealth. Once their target level of wealth is obtained, many individuals suspend active saving.[14] Saving rates have fallen over the past 30 years while the capital gains tax rate has fallen from 28% in 1987 to 15% today (0% for taxpayers in the 10% and 15% tax brackets). This suggests that changing capital gains tax rates have had little effect on private saving.

Some have argued that preferential capital gains tax rates will boost high risk investments such as in venture capital. Most venture capital, however, is supplied by pension funds, college endowments, foundations, and insurance companies—sources not associated with the capital gains tax. In 2003, only about 10% of investors in venture capital funds were individuals and families.[15]

Additionally, for risk adverse investors, the capital gains tax could act as an insurance for risky investments by reducing losses as well as gains—it decreases the variability of returns.[16] The $3,000 loss limit may reduce the insurance value of the capital gains tax. But research has shown that almost three-quarters of taxpayers with capital losses were not subject to the loss limit because losses were less than $3,000 or gains offset the losses.[17] Of those affected by the loss limit, two-thirds were able to deduct losses against gains or other income within two years. The capital gains tax, therefore, may have little effect on risk-taking and may even encourage it.

Capital gains tax rate reductions appear to decrease public saving and may have little or no effect on private saving. Consequently, capital gains tax reductions likely have a negative overall impact on national saving.

Economic Growth

Some have argued that reducing capital gains tax rates would increase short-run and long-run economic growth.[18] The long-run level of output depends on the amount of saving and investment. Saving and investment increase the amount of capital in the economy and hence, aggregate supply (i.e., the amount of goods and services available in the economy). Many economists note that capital gains tax reductions appear to have little or even a negative effect on saving and investment (see above). Consequently, capital gains tax rate reductions are unlikely to have much effect on the long-term level of output or the path to the long-run level of output (i.e., economic growth).

Furthermore, it is argued that a temporary or permanent capital gains tax reduction is an effective economic stimulus measure. An effective short-term economic stimulus, however, will have to increase aggregate demand, which requires additional spending. A tax reduction on capital gains would mostly benefit very high income taxpayers who are likely to save most of any tax reduction.[19] Economists note that a temporary capital gains tax reduction possibly could have a negative impact on short-term economic growth. A temporary tax cut could induce investors to sell stock (i.e., realize capital gains by reducing the lock-in effect), but provides no incentive to invest since investors know they will face higher tax rates in the future. To the extent that the resulting sell-off depresses stock prices, consumer confidence, already low during recessions, could be further undermined thus reducing consumer spending.

A permanent capital gains tax cut will likely have two offsetting effects on stock prices. There is the demand-side capitalization effect—investors would be willing to pay a higher price for assets on which they would pay lower capital gains taxes in the future (in essence shifting out the demand curve). But there is also the supply-side lock-in effect in which investors would be willing to sell at a lower price because they have to pay lower capital gains taxes (in essence shifting out the supply curve). The ultimate effect on stock returns depends on the relative magnitude of these two effects, but it would likely be small in either direction.

Appendix. Data Sources

Two data sources are used in the analysis. The first is the 2007 Survey of Consumer Finances (SCF), which is prepared by the Federal Reserve Board. The SCF includes detailed information on household demographics, income, and wealth. In the analysis, households are ranked in the income distribution and assigned to income categories (quintiles) by their equivalence-adjusted household income, which is household income divided by the square root of family size. Each income quintile contains 20% of the households; in addition, the richest 10% (decile) and richest 5% (ventile) are included in the analysis. This adjustment controls for economies of scale within the household. Household income consists of income from all sources including public assistance, but excludes capital gains. All households are represented in the SCF sample regardless of whether or not they paid taxes.

Some analysts argue that capital gains income can temporarily make a low or moderate income household appear rich. To the extent that this is true, most capital gains income will appear to be received solely by the rich. Consequently, capital gains income is excluded from household income when assigning households to income categories. Most individuals and families, however, are in the same income category regardless of capital gains income—92% remain in the same quintile and 77% remain in the same ventile.

The second data source is the IRS's 2004 Statistics of Income Public Use File (SOI PUF). The SOI PUF contains information from the tax returns of a representative sample of taxpayers. Individuals and families that do not file a tax return are not included in this data source. These individuals and families are not required to file a tax return because of low income or receive primarily nontaxable income (e.g., public assistance). Taxpayers are assigned to income categories based on equivalence-adjusted total income; total income excludes capital gains income.

End Notes

[1] See Henry C. Simons, *Personal Income Taxation* (Chicago: University of Chicago Press, 1938).

[2] Capital assets are defined in Section 1221 of the Internal Revenue Code and explained in IRS publication 544. IRS publication 544 (p. 19) simply states that "[a]lmost everything you own and use for personal purposes or investment is a capital asset."

[3] See CRS Report RL31562, *An Analysis of the Tax Treatment of Capital Losses*, by Thomas L. Hungerford and Jane G. Gravelle.

[4] Martin Feldstein, Joel Slemrod, and Shlomo Yitzhaki, "The Effects of Taxation on the Selling of Corporate Stock and the Realizations of Capital Gains," *Quarterly Journal of Economics*, vol. 94, no. 4 (June 1980), p. 790.

[5] The authors note the problem of using cross-sectional data: "An individual whose tax rate varies substantially from year to year will tend to sell more when his rate is low. To the extent that low rates in 1973 are only temporarily low, our estimates will overstate the sensitivity of selling to the tax rate. We have no way of knowing how important this is" (p. 785).

[6] See Leonard E. Burman, *Labyrinth of Capital Gains Tax Policy: A Guide for the Perplexed* (Washington: Brookings Institution Press, 1999) and Jane G. Gravelle, *The Economic Effects of Taxing Capital Income* (Cambridge, MA: MIT Press, 1994) for discussions of this issue.

[7] Alan J. Auerbach, "Capital Gains Taxation and Tax Reform," *National Tax Journal*, vol. 42, no. 3 (1989), pp. 391-401. Auerbach concludes that "a permanent revenue increase [from a capital gains tax rate reduction] is unlikely enough to be discarded as a reason for reducing the capital gains tax rate" (p. 391).

[8] Jane G. Gravelle, "Limits to Capital Gains Feedback Effects," *Tax Notes*, vol. 51 (April 22, 1991), pp. 363-371.

[9] Gerald E. Auten and Charles T. Clotfelter, "Permanent versus Transitory Tax Effects and the Realization of Capital Gains," *Quarterly Journal of Economics*, vol. 97, no. 4 (November 1982), pp. 613-632.

[10] Leonard E. Burman and William C. Randolph, "Measuring Permanent Responses to Capital-Gains Tax Changes in Panel Data," *American Economic Review*, vol. 84, no. 4 (September 1994), pp. 794-809.

[11] The 2007 SCF doesn't allow capital gains accruals for other assets to be calculated.

[12] See Jane G. Gravelle, "Can A Capital Gains Tax Cut Pay for Itself," *Tax Notes*, vol. 48 (July 9, 1990), pp. 209-219.

[13] For a discussion and citations to the literature see CRS Report RL33482, *Saving Incentives: What May Work, What May Not*, by Thomas L. Hungerford.

[14] F. Thomas Juster, Joseph P. Lupton, James P. Smith, and Frank Stafford, "The Decline in Household Saving and the Wealth Effect," *Review of Economics and Statistics*, vol. 87, no. 4 (November 2005), pp. 20-27.

[15] National Venture Capital Association, *Venture Impact*, 4th Edition, 2007, available at http://www.nvca.org/pdf/ NVCA_VentureCapital07-2nd.pdf.

[16] See Burman, *Labyrinth of Capital Gains Tax Policy*.

[17] Alan J. Auerbach, Leonard E. Burman, and Jonathan M. Siegel, "Capital Gains Taxation and Tax Avoidance: New Evidence from Panel Data," in *Does Atlas Shrug?* ed. Joel B. Slemrod (Cambridge, MA: Harvard University Press, 2000), pp. 355-388.

[18] See, for example, Karen A. Campbell and Guinevere Nell, *Sustainable Economic Stimulus: Repeal Capital Gains and Dividend Taxes*, The Heritage Foundation, Web Memo no. 2263, February 3, 2009.

[19] See Jonathan McCarthy, "Imperfect Insurance and Differing Propensities to Consume Across Households," *Journal of Monetary Economics*, vol. 36, no. 2 (November 1995), pp. 301-327 for evidence that the wealthy have higher marginal propensities to save than low wealth households.

INDEX

N

O

P

R

S

T

U

V